JUICING
Therapy

by
Bernard Jensen, Ph.D.

PUBLISHED BY:

Bernard Jensen, Ph.D.
24360 Old Wagon Road
Escondido, CA 92027 USA

This book, in any way or form, is not meant to give specific recommendations and/or advice for the treatment of particular diseases or illnesses, nor is it intended to be a replacement for good, competent medical diagnosis and/or treatment. The reader is strongly cautioned against self-treatment and strongly urged to seek the help and guidance of a licensed, competent health-care professional whenever necessary.

Because there is always some risk involved, the author/publisher is not responsible for any adverse effects or consequences from the use of any of the suggestions, preparations or procedures in this book. Please do not use this book if you are unwilling to assume the risk. Always consult a physician or other qualified health professional if you have any questions concerning information given in this book. It is a sign of wisdom, not cowardice, to seek a second or third opinion.

Nothing in this book is to be construed as, or to take the place of appropriate medical advice, diagnosis or treatment. The skilled services of competent, health professionals should always be consulted when conditions warrant.

First Edition
Copyright 1992 Bernard Jensen

ISBN 0-932615-27-9

BERNARD JENSEN, Publisher
24360 Old Wagon Road
Escondido, CA 92027 USA

What's in This Book!!

—Nutritional wisdom that can save your life!

—Case histories of people healed after using juice therapy

—Wonderful juice combination recipes

—Special section on liquefied foods

—Delicious, health-building blender recipes

—Supplements to add to blender drinks

—How nature heals body organs and systems

—Why we must treat the patient, not the disease

—The chemical story you need to know

—Juices for babies and children

—Soups from juices and blender combinations

—Herbs and green drinks

—Wonderful salad dressings

—Best veggies and fruits to use

—Vitamins and minerals and where to find them

—Special "Analytical Food Guide" chart.

Let's drink for health!

*The necessary therapy may be in the juices
to reclaim and maintain our health.*

—Dr. Bernard Jensen

CONTENTS

Preface

I was introduced to the healing power of juices early in my
career when a woman about 30 years old came to my office
with 13 leg ulcers, several the size of silver dollars, open and
running pus. Three years of treatments by several doctors had
not helped her.

She had been examined and treated at two of the top medical
clinics in the United States. At one of them, she was treated for
hypocalcemia, a shortage of calcium, which her doctor believed
to be part of her problem. He prescribed drugstore calcium,
which she could not assimilate. This little lady was getting very
discouraged when someone told her about my work as a clinical
nutritionist.

As I listened to her story, I couldn't help but wonder how I
was going to assist a person that so many other doctors had
tried to help and failed. Then I thought of the elderly Hunza
people who still had every tooth in their heads, strong bones
and healthy skin at ages over a hundred years. Where did they
get their calcium? Why did they have such good calcium
control? It most certainly was partly due to the fresh greens
they ate.

Fresh greens are high in the vitamin A precursor, carotene,
which helps control calcium in the body. And, greens also
contain a significant amount of calcium. So, I thought, if I
could get her to drink juice from several different kinds of
green vegetables, maybe it would speed up the healing of the
leg ulcers. She would be getting an easily assimilated natural
form of calcium in the juice, and she would also be getting
enough vitamin A to control the distribution in the body.

I believe in putting my patients to work so they are involved
in their own healing processes. I had the woman with the leg
ulcers chopping up green leafy vegetables on a cutting board
day after day—spinach, dandelion greens, kale and I don't

1

know how many others. We would soak them in water until all the good green juices had "bled" into the water, then strain it through cheesecloth. And, she would drink this green vegetable juice diluted in water, a glass every hour, all day. She had pellagra, which is a lack of calcium. I am convinced that greens control calcium in the body.

It was hard work, but it paid off. In three weeks, the thirteen leg ulcers were completely healed. The secret was in the juice! What prescription remedies from drugstores failed to cure, mother nature completely healed.

I want to bring attention to the chlorophyll in the green leafy vegetable juice, because I am certain that it played an important role in the healing process, too. Chlorophyll is the life-blood of plants, one of the most wonderful blood cleansers I have ever used with patients. It cleanses the blood by cleansing the bowel of those toxins most commonly assimilated into the bloodstream. "When you're green inside, you're clean inside," I always told my patients. Experience has demonstrated to me the value of keeping the bowel clean by means of chlorophyll-rich drinks. A clean bowel helps prevent disease.

The success of this case and hundreds like it eventually established my reputation—and increased any confidence in what I was bringing into my patients' lives and bodies. I enjoy seeing people improve in their health, and juices are a wonderful source of nutrients that I believe we all need to take advantage of to reach for the highest level of health and well-being we can get.

Juices (and other liquids) are the fastest method I know for getting nutrients—in easily-digested and assimilated form—into the blood and lymph systems that feed the cells and maintain the body's health.

We find out that fruit juices tend to supply more of the vitamins, while vegetable juices tend to supply more minerals, although each has both. Freshness and ripeness are factors that influence the nutritional value of the fruits and vegetables we run through our juicers, but soil is by far the most important influence. Juice should be used soon after being made.

If the soil is depleted of important minerals, the fruit and vegetables grown from that soil will be depleted of those same minerals. The label "organic" on a fruit or vegetable doesn't guarantee that it has been grown on mineral-rich soil, so we need to do a certain amount of research and investigation to find out where the fruits and vegetables we purchase are grown, and what the quality of the soil is in that place.

I want to make clear that I don't believe we can make a life on juices—we need fiber foods for bowel tone and proper elimination, including whole grains, raw nuts and seeds, and sources of protein such as eggs, cheese and yogurt. A juice diet is not a balanced diet, but there may be times when a juice fast is appropriate for certain physical ailments and conditions, and I'll discuss them in this book.

In my own nutritional regimen, I use juices much the same as I use supplements—to get specific nutrients into the body fast so they can get to the cells and restore proper function and balance. The vitamins, minerals and enzymes present in juices are able to be assimilated and launched into the bloodstream or lymph system much faster than if solid food had been taken.

I believe in juices. I believe we can easily include a juice snack in our diets twice a day for better health and well-being, and for an extra measure of protection from disease. I want to emphasize the need for variety in the kinds of juices we use, because variety is the only way we can be sure of getting all the different nutrients we need every day.

If you want to feel better and live longer, juicing and juices are for you.

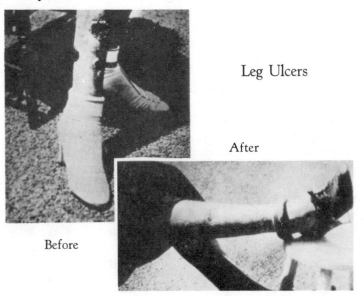

Leg Ulcers

After

Before

Introduction

This little book can bring you back to life if you pay close attention to what you are reading, and if you become "doers of the word, and not hearers only! It can save you from collapsing into an early grave and may greatly reduce the amount of money you invest in your family physician.

Since I've written a highly-favorable Foreword to Stephen Blauer's *The Juicing Book,* it will come as no surprise to anyone that I very much approve of juicing and believe in the health benefits of fresh juices. I also believe Stephen Blauer has written a very fine book on the subject and I encourage you to get your copy.

We must learn the simple truth, that we don't (and can't) heal a disease. It is the patient we should be taking care of, not the diseases, and we take a giant step forward in our own understanding and perspective when we recognize that juices are great health builders, but they are not "medications" prescribed to alleviate or suppress disease symptoms.

Your life and life depend on what is in this book.

Nutrition has always been the foundational healing art, absolutely necessary before any kind of healing can take place in the body. How can I say this? Because only the chemical elements can rebuild cells or correct defects in cells, and because our ultimate source of chemical elements is foods, the success of all other healing arts depends on **this one healing art**.

We need to get it into our heads **that foods have the chemicals needed for tissue repair**. Foods, including juices, build tissue, and when a sufficient amount of cleansing and building has taken place, the body heals itself by virtue of natural laws.

Hippocrates once said, "We will never understand disease until we understand foods." He meant the makeup of foods, the chemical elements needed for repair and rebuilding. He had no idea of the micronutrients in foods, the chemical elements. But he knew foods played a part in preparing a body for healing.

I have visited the island of Kos where Hippocrates was born and raised, and I can tell you, we need to learn to get the most out of our foods. Hippocrates said, "Foods should be our medicine, and our medicine should be foods." We need to inform ourselves about the foods available in our own corner of the world and learn what those foods can and cannot do for us.

People with seriously compromised health may have to use supplements and juices quite a lot at first, but our objective should always be to work toward a balanced regimen of whole, pure and natural foods, like my Health and Harmony Food Regimen. I want to note here that juices are foods, not supplements in the usual understanding of the word.

It is important for you and everyone who wants better health to begin taking greater responsibility for our own health, and in this book, I will share some very nice ways of doing this. We have to care about staying healthy, or who will care for us?

We find that disease can come when you don't care, when you don't have the proper foods going into your body, when you are living on foods that man has handled and hasn't put the care in it that he should have in order to keep it natural, pure, fresh and whole.

Dr. V.G. Rocine was my greatest teacher, my greatest mentor. He taught me how to find the chemical elements in foods. You find this idea in one of my greatest books, *Foods That Heal.* This approach is taken after Hippocrates and Rocine. This tells you how to get the chemical elements you need. If you have to make juices out of foods that are high in calcium, go at it and do it and if you have to get greens, find out what greens you can use, juice them and get them into that body as soon as you can. Better health begins the day you start.

Next day, however, it hasn't all arrived, but a start has been made. You never felt the first problem that started in your body. You'll never hear, feel, see what one single salad will do for you, but if you have a salad every day for a year, you'll know that it does good for you.

If you have juices, if you can have them every day for a year as a supplement to your regular foods, I believe you will be delighted at the improvement in your well-being that takes place.

I visited the isolated Hunza Valley in Pakistan many years ago to find out for myself if the people were as disease-free and lived as long as Dr. Robert McCarrison reported in the early part of this century. In a world which seems to be constantly on the verge of being overwhelmed by disease, the residents of the Hunza Valley were a refreshing contrast. There were no jails, hospitals, policemen or doctors. Why? Because the people were healthy and well-balanced mentally and socially, in a high Himalayan Valley where the corrupt foods, customs and manners of civilization could not easily reach them, and where they had to live off of the simple foods they grew on rich, glacier-watered soil. Cancer, heart disease, diabetes, kidney disease, arthritis were unknown by the residents of Hunza while I was there.

The food we eat and the lifestyle we live have a great deal of influence over our health and longevity. Some of the Hunzakuts I met were over 120 years old and still had all their teeth, smooth skin, clear eyes, good memories and were able to walk for miles to work in the fields or visit friends and relatives. The Hunza diet was high in natural carbohydrates and low in protein. They walked up and down steep mountain roads and trails every day. I didn't see anyone overweight because their meals were generally sparse, although rich in nutritional value.

It is possible to learn from and imitate parts of the Hunza lifestyle, to our benefit, for longer life and better health, and juices should be an everyday part of our program.

It is my responsibility to urge you to be cautious about juices and use your head about how extreme to go. I don't think you should go off and live for 60 days on carrot juice or 45 days on orange juice. Any juice fast should be discussed with your doctor, and possibly overseen by him. Always discuss any unusual health idea with your doctor before you consider action on it.

A lot of minerals are locked up in the fibers of some of the foods that we can take and juicing removes them. Vegetable juices are one of the great ways of getting these minerals back into our bodies. **Juices are natural foods.**

Juicing is a nonconventional therapy. It's an alternative therapy that works in the body and can strengthen the body to begin reversing a disease. Juicing saturates the tissues with wonderful vitamins, minerals and enzymes, enabling the tissue to throw off encumbrances in good time.

One of the ways we know that diet makes a significant impact on our health and longevity is because studies have been done on the Seventh Day Adventists, a Christian denomination committed to a largely vegetarian diet. The overwhelming majority do not use alcohol, tobacco or drugs. They have almost no incidence of lung cancer, and their statistics on cancer, in general, and heart disease show they have much less of these killer diseases than other Americans. In fact, they seem to have less trouble with all diseases than the general population. They use a balanced approach to diet.

I met an old man in the Caucasus mountains of the former USSR whose name was Gassanoff. He was 153 years of age. They put us on television in Moscow, and I asked him, "What rules have you used for living 153 years" He said, "I didn't know I was going to get to 153 years, so I have no rules."

People are under a lot of rules these days. They say there are 365,000 laws on the books today to enforce the Ten Commandments.

Let's learn how to live; let's find out what the proper lifestyle is and let's follow God's laws more than the politicians. Those who are trying to legislate us into poor health and wellness rules are making a sad mistake. They could even be responsible for some of the diseases we are manifesting today.

There should be a basic science that describes tissue changes, and we should have grants that give us an education that tells us what foods make the proper tissue changes. We should have an examination and we should have testimonials of what can be done. They haven't any laboratory test to tell these things yet. When they tell you you're short of calcium, they give chalk calcium to replace that bio-organic calcium. It's not a food, not a biochemic food, and it should never enter into the body.

We know so little about food and the laws of nature, that no wonder we have nothing to go ahead of us to make sure our way. We haven't any influence on most people.

If we're going to be gentle and flexible in taking care of people these days, we've got to recognize that nutrition and juices are a slow, subtle therapy. Juices aren't addictive. They don't have undesirable side effects unless you overeat or undereat too long. There's no side effects from foods.

CHEMICAL REPLACEMENT STORY

Don't expect immediate results from juice therapy. Immediate results will not come to you. This is a flowing situation. This is a gentle art of healing. I tell my patients it takes at least a year before they can get well on the proper foods. So we've got to find out where this therapy comes in.

Juicing, taken from a doctor's perspective, is a supplementary therapy to be used with a balanced diet such as my Health and Harmony Food Regimen. It should not be used by itself unless under a doctor's supervision. A juice diet is dangerous in the hands of an inexperienced person when using for a prolonged period.

My approach to reversal of disease or prevention of disease could be called replacement therapy. We have to replace the old, damaged tissue with healthy, new tissue. We do this by providing the body with a slight excess of chemical elements in our food regimen, to take care of longstanding or short-term deficiencies.

When the constitutionally weak tissues are cleansed and strengthened, the whole body participates in a three-to-five-day healing crisis, throwing off old catarrh and toxic encumbrances and building healthy new tissue. This is what natural healing is all about. We don't heal. We take care of chemical deficiencies and the body heals itself.

This is a wonderful book full of wonderful ideas about juicing, liquefying and cultivating wellness. Enjoy it, and use it with wisdom.

SECTION I

JUICE THERAPY:
How to Use Juices Successfully

CHAPTER ONE

A DOCTOR VIEWS JUICE THERAPY

Much has been said about juicing, about taking the vital liquids from the fibers of fruits, vegetables, nuts and so forth, and many people don't realize that these all belong to nature. It may surprise you to learn that nature does not cure diseases. We find out that everybody today wants to be a doctor. Everybody wants to cure a disease.

Treating a disease is not the way to get a new body. Nature's way is through rebuilding the chemical structure of damaged tissue. *From the dust of the earth thou art and to dust thou shall return,* the Good Book says. We are constantly in a state of change where chemicals are coming into the body and going out of the body. There's no such thing as disease in a body which has all the chemical elements in good balance and sufficient supply. Disease does not live in that kind of tissue. We find that diseases only live in damaged tissue, a devitalized tissue that comes from devitalized food or from empty calorie food that doesn't have the mineral elements we need. We are living on a starving diet.

All diseases are a sign of starvation. The good news about juicing is that it is a wonderful source of minerals.

THE CHEMICAL STORY IS YOUR STORY

When it comes to the chemical story, we find out this is the most important lesson a person can learn. Nature will set you straight if you let her. And she can do it, but she needs the opportunity.

People who live on junk foods, only get a junk body. If you eat "half a loaf" of bread from a nutrition standpoint, you only get half the value. For example, in the case of white bread that runs 25% less calcium than whole wheat bread, you're going to get shorted. As a result, you're going to develop bone diseases, decayed teeth and conditions like osteomyelitis and osteoporosis. You're going to have all kinds of mental problems with a calcium-depleted diet. You're going to have fear problems, confusion, uncertainty, indecision, depression and other problems you can't control. The mind is always influenced by our body chemistry. When the chemistry is wrong, the mind suffers as well as the body.

Calcium is one of the elements that makes us strong, gives us power, grounds us, keeps us moving, allows us to press forward and keeps us from being wilted daisies in our activities. So, let's get the calcium back into the body. And you can only do it when you have the calcium-rich foods—the whole grains, raw nuts and seeds, green, leafy vegetables (kale is highest in calcium); so that you can have a body molded to the proper foods. Juices from kale and other green, leafy vegetables can increase our calcium intake.

Our food intake quality is very important. It's time we recognize that food intake is "on the other end" of every symptom in the body. There is no disease that isn't accompanied by a chemical shortage, and it is time we realize that if these chemical shortages are taken care of, we wouldn't be treating a disease. Juicing helps build the whole body by providing a rich supply of chemical elements.

DON'T BE MISLED—THE TRUTH
IS GOOD ENOUGH FOR ALL OF US

Let us get off the ideas now that juices are going to cure diabetes, that juices are going to cure cancer, that juices are going to cure anything! What we are going to do is work with nature, and nature will do the curing. And, yes, we use juices as part of our program. Nature is self-building, self-repairing, self-rejuvenating, and you rebuild, repair and rejuvenate automatically when you sleep, when you're not even conscious. We find that when we are working too hard, we break down our bodies through mental efforts. The nervous system is going to come out short if you don't have the proper balance in your lifestyle. Juices help.

We can become chemically deficient in any of the different systems in our body. That deficiency affects the various functions in the respiratory system, in the urinary system, in the glandular system. What do you suppose will happen if we do not have the nutrients to replace those used up in the brain during the day? What happens when we use up the body's chemical elements? We become chemically short, the body malfunctions and then we treat these symptoms as a disease. I want you to know that every disease is a definite sign of chemical shortages somewhere in the body. Nature cures, and the juices that nature provides can prevent or reverse the chemical shortages that give disease a foothold in the body. The Bircher-Benner Institute in Zurich, Switzerland, was trying to help their worst and most hopeless cases with raw juices and raw foods. I saw such wonderful changes in some of their patients that I could hardly believe my eyes.

I am not the only doctor who realizes this, but I'll tell you, it's taken 65 years of sanitarium practice to confirm that when we replenish the chemical elements in a person through vegetable juices, fruit juices and through liquids and supplements, along with a balanced diet, good health is restored.

In my work, many diseases respond to improved diet. I can show you many case histories where diabetic people improve and don't have to use as much insulin as before because of changing to juices, liquid chlorophyll and other nutrients to bring the proper chemical balance to their body. I have seen open, running leg ulcers healed. I've seen people make wonderful changes in their body when they are fed properly. I consider juice as a food.

FOODS ARE NOT MEDICINES

I am totally committed to treating people through proper nutrition, but the first thing I want you to realize is that the foods are not doing the curing, they're only assuring that you have all that nature needs in order to make a good body. We never see a sore get well. You never see a cut heal. These are done automatically when the right nutrients are available. When they aren't available, sores, poor skin conditions, ulcers, respiratory troubles, asthma, hay fever, emphysema and all of our diseases—from the acute to the chronic—linger on. We must have the chemical material to make what we need to be healthy, well, active, vigorous and strong enough to do our jobs, to have good marriages and to take care of all the challenges that come along in life.

I consider fresh fruit and vegetable juices one of the very best ways of making sure we have the fitness and good health to take care of life's challenges.

I have been working with clinical nutrition now for many years and have seen many wonderful results, but I don't have the laboratory tests to prove that complete tissue restoration, complete healing takes place. However, there's hardly a case that comes in that I don't have some medical laboratory tests showing improvements when patients are fed properly and when nutritients are resupplied to the body after long-term deficiencies.

DOCTORS MAKE A LIVING ON YOUR LIVING

It is this neglect of nutrition that doctors make their living on. It is due to this neglect that we find all kinds of symptoms—16,000 symptoms and symptom combinations have been recorded for the different ailments, disturbances and diseases including insomnia, shortness of breath, heart arrhythmia, bowel pockets, rickets, bowel toxemia and so on. You can go right down the line, and every single one of these symptoms can be helped with nutritional means, especially through the use of fresh fruit and vegetable juices.

It is time to realize that it isn't a perfect laboratory test that determines whether a patient is well, but rather, actual changes in the person's body, sense of well-being and energy level. Is the patient feeling better? Is he still on medication? Is his level of physical activity up to what it used to be? We shouldn't be satisfied with only symptom relief, where you and your doctor are just coddling the disease and the symptoms. That way, you will end up in surgery or in a rest home. You will end up at the end of your life unable to work and having to be cared for by someone else.

We find out that our greatest reservoir of wisdom is in the elderly people in our nation. Yet, we do not take care of the elderly properly. We cannot have good health at the end of our life if we don't start at a younger age. We find that what you do today and tomorrow can still have its effects 10 years from now. Or, why would the Cancer Society tell you it takes 20 years to build some types of cancer? Where was the doctor in the beginning? Are people using any preventive means? It's a temporary visit that we're having in this physical body, and it's going to be *very* temporary if we don't use the right nutritional support. The older we become, the more valuable juices become because they are easily digested and assimilated.

It is time to replenish that body of yours with everything you possibly can. I'll tell you about one of the greatest ways I know to do it.

VEGETABLE JUICE THERAPY

In the vegetable juice therapy, it's not a matter of applying a cure to a disease. Just make sure you have the proper understanding of what is going on.

What we are doing with vegetable juice therapy is to transfer vital minerals—as dissolved in juices, into the body and its fluids (blood and lymph). This starts a cleansing process. First, the lymph stream cannot be clean unless we have the proper minerals going to that lymph stream. If lymph is clouded with toxic material, if it is polluted with chemical toxins from bad air, bad water, food additives, poison sprays that have been used on foods and radiation that has altered the chemistry of the food, we cannot expect the lymph system to do its job of cleansing the body and protecting it against germ life.

The best cleansing that I possibly can think of is by using the mineral-rich vegetable and fruit juices. If we could put pure water into our bodies that was loaded with bio-organic calcium (not the calcium oxalate that is found in heavily-laden spring waters), we would start a cleansing process.

JUICES ARE MOSTLY FOR CLEANSING

We need to have equal amounts of cleansing and building in the body. It should be a 50/50 proposition. If you're going to go through a 75 percent elimination and 25 percent building, program, you're on a diet. Junk foods can make up a "diet" just as going on grape juice entirely may be considered as a "diet." Going on carrot juice entirely is a diet. We have to eventually get back to a healthy way of living. And our Health and Harmony diet is the thing you must always work for. A truly balanced diet is always half cleansing (removing undesirable toxins and catarrh from the tissues) and half building (repairing and restoring tissue integrity).

People underestimate the potency and effectiveness of juices. Dr. H.E. Kirschner of Valley View Sanitarium in Los Angeles came to see me one time about a patient of mine who had cured himself of a terminal disease by taking only carrot juice for over a year. Dr. Kirschner was a medical doctor who believed in the healing power of foods. The doctor has talked to my patient, Mr. Del Wilhite of Azusa, California, and was convinced of the truthfulness of his story, and he came to me for my side of it.

I told him, "Del came to me after his doctors had given him up. He had been diagnosed as having a degenerative condition in the bowel and could hardly eat anything. I put him on carrot juice, because nearly anyone can take it, and it agreed well with him. He had lost a good deal of weight, but what he had left stabilized after he began taking the carrot juice, or a little liquid chlorophyll. He passed some unbelievable material from his bowel during the course of his juice fast, and at the end of the year, he went back to the hospital for a checkup. *His hospital report proved that he was absolutely free of the terminal disease!* This was a very wonderful thing for him, and, of course, he was overjoyed. He was able to go back to a regimen of solid foods, but he was careful to use whole, pure and natural foods to make sure he kept his healing."

Dr. Kirschner was so impressed with this case that he wrote an article about it and sent it to a medical journal to show what juices could for a person. The article was returned to him along with a note saying the story lacked credibility and that it wasn't up to the medical profession to promote any food for the healing of any disease. Dr. Kirschner said, "I have visited this man and I can hardly believe the good health he is in. I believe his story."

Dr. Kirschner developed his own organic garden in Yucaipa, where vegetables and herbs were raised for his patients. He believed in natural healing through foods and juices and wrote several books about his successes with patients. I'll have more to say about him later in this book.

More recently, beta carotene (which is very high in carrots) has been tested with laboratory rats and mice and has been shown to prevent or reverse certain types of cancers induced in these laboratory animals. Research into the anticarcinogenic properties of beta carotene (pro-vitamin A) are continuing. These are university tests and in the medical departments.

THE PLACE OF VEGETABLE JUICES

The function that vegetable juices provide best is to help balance a diet that emphasizes more building than it should. Such a diet over stresses protein and starches with not enough of the vegetable eliminating properties. To replace any damaged cells in the body, it is necessary that our juices contain the chemical elements required to build new molecular structures. This takes vital fluids and liquids that transmit the vital energies of the sun, air and water so they can reach every cell in the body.

Cells in the body have a very close connection with the blood. The blood visits every cell in the body. And you'll find that if the blood is going to be the life in your body, and you're going to live on the blood that flows through your body, you must take care of that blood. Saturate it with vitamins, enzymes and minerals from all the vegetable juices you can as far as an elimination goes, but using good sense with it. It is possible that some people can go on just vegetable juices. That's a vegetable juice diet, as we have mentioned before. Personally, I feel that the vegetable juices and fruit juices should be used as a supplement to the regular diet in the average person. If you're going to go on these vegetable juices, fruit juices, nut juices, nut drinks and so forth, consider that they are a special dieting procedure.

SPECIAL DIETING PROCEDURES DO WHAT?

First of all, special diets may be tailored to restore chemical balance to the body structures you have weakened the last 20 years or so by wrong food and lifestyle habits. It's not what you eat that counts, it's what you digest. You must chew your food adequately. You must take care of your gastrointestinal system. You must exercise enough to force the circulating blood to visit and feed every cell in the body. Juicing forces out the vital juices that come within the fruit and vegetable fibers. Is it possible that trace minerals dissolved in those juices could be used in various parts of the body? Why is it that the trace minerals selenium, boron and zinc are selling so well in the health food stores when you get a good deal of them in freshly juiced vegetable juices?

Vegetable juices will help compensate for what you didn't eat years ago. Think on this! It isn't what you eat, many times, it's what you didn't eat. You starved yourself. Did you get enough zinc? Did you get enough selenium? How about the boron? When the boron isn't in the soil, the leaves of avocado trees turn brown and begin to drop off. Farmers call it a disease, and we begin to see these diseases come on when the soil lacks certain minerals needed to give the tree all the health it should have. You have to find these things out. I'm not telling you anything new. (Refer to a book titled *Empty Harvest* by Bernard Jensen and Mark Anderson.)

Orchard trees have been found to develop disease symptoms when certain minerals are lacking in the soil, just as people do when certain minerals are lacking in their foods.

We must take care of the soil, we must take care of the blood, we must take care of the nutrients which must be delivered to every organ in the body. We do this by taking in the proper chemical elements and having them in abundance, as found in juices.

THE ABUNDANCE OF THE CHEMICAL ELEMENTS
IN THE VEGETABLE JUICES

We find that nutrients soluble in juices are easiest to take in the body. When we are sick, when we develop diseases and have no vitality, no energy, no pick up and go, we do not digest or assimilate foods well. A tired, fatigued body does not get much value from foods taken in.

We tend to run our bodies down to a frazzle. We've been vitality wasters. We haven't left any nerve energy for our digestive tract to get the good out of some of the foods we're eating, such as fast foods, heavy cold starches, cold beans and foods altered by preservation methods, cooking, frying, demineralizing, etc. Trace minerals are also necessary.

PREPARE YOUR FOOD FOR EASY DIGESTION

Vegetable juices, fruit juices and liquefied foods are more easily digested than solid foods, raw or cooked. It is not what you eat, many times, but what you absorb, and if you don't absorb the mineral elements from your foods, you're going to end up in chemical shortages.

I have often mentioned how effectively our natural food program has been over the years in my sanitarium work, where over 100,000 patients have been blessed by a food regimen which emphasized vegetable juices. We grew 3,000 pounds of carrots (and other vegetables) a month just to make vegetable juices every morning at 10 o'clock for our patients. Since we cared, we grew the vegetables. Since we cared, we served vegetable juices to our patients. If you care, you should use organic vegetable juices. The life you save may be your own.

STATEMENTS WRITTEN BY ONE OF
OUR GREAT MEDICAL DOCTORS, DR. TOM SPIES

Dr. Tom Spies was honored by the American Medical Association in 1957 for his great contribution to the healing art through his work with foods. Here is how he summed up his findings.

All diseases are caused by chemicals. All diseases can be cured by chemicals. All the chemicals used by the body except for the oxygen which we breathe and the water which we drink are taken in through food. If we only knew enough, all diseases could be prevented and could be cured through proper nutrition.

As tissues become damaged, they lack the chemicals for good nutrition. They tend to become old. They lack what I call "tissue integrity." There are people of 40 whose brains and arteries are senile. If we could help the tissues repair themselves by correcting nutritional deficiencies, we can make old age wait.

How did he ever come to these conclusions? There's hope and inspiration in this doctor who opened his eyes and took a different viewpoint. The wise man is always willing to consider the potential value of an alternative view. Is there another way of taking care of our problems in life?

IT HURTS TO BE ON THE CUTTING EDGE

How do you suppose a person like me felt when I saw the heading of a newspaper several years ago stating they have now found that vegetables are good for preventing cancer? That less insulin is needed by diabetics when they use the proper foods? That birth defects in children can be avoided when mothers use a balanced diet during pregnancy? What a great thing it would be if we were willing to assure ourselves of having healthy children by looking carefully after our own health 20 years before they were conceived.

Don't blame the mothers and fathers. We have to blame the doctors who know better but haven't taught us how to live properly. We have the medication, but we do not have the education. The latter has sorely been neglected and, unless that is changed, we're not going to have the better things in life.

LET'S LOOK AT THE "LIFE FACTOR"

The picture below shows seeds found in King Tut's tomb. They are 2,000 years old. Some were planted and they grew! It's that "life factor" in the foods we need. We have to have "live" foods.

Seeds from King Tut's tomb.

21

The first planting of the seeds from King Tut's tomb was in England. The first of these peas were eaten on January 19, 1945, and proved to have a very appetizing flavor.

It is almost a miracle that these seeds grew after 2,000 years! There's a hull protecting them. Nothing can destroy the fertility of seeds unless the hull is penetrated or fractured.

Similarly, the greatest thing I can tell you is that in juicing and in liquefying, you have the opportunity of breaking down and "fracturizing" the cells and tissues of vegetables, getting the juices out with the "life factor" intact. It is this "life factor" that makes juices such a wonderfully valuable supplement to a balanced diet.

To get this vital material into our body, our foods have to be alive. In some of the 200-year-old monasteries in Florida, they found flower seeds, planted them and they grew. Why? Nature is interested in the next generation. She's so interested she produces a protective hull around seeds and a protective membrane around cells containing vegetable juices.

Some vegetables, nuts and seeds contain the high-powered principles and chemical activities that are needed to renew glands, such as the pituitary, thyroid, adrenals, prostate, ovaries, testes and so on. When we take in the "gland-building factors," we help the whole body. This is not taking care of the disease, this is taking care of the chemical deficiencies. And this is what vegetable juices and liquefied foods should be used for. This is one of the reasons we should get live foods.

In a microwave oven, you can cook wheat, but if you put it in the ground after it is cooked, it will not grow. It is dead as a door nail. And you find out it's the life in these foods that is so very important. But if you cook that same kind of wheat in stainless steel, low-heat cooking utensils, when that wheat is done, it can be planted in the ground and it will grow. Not enough heat has been applied to it to kill the germ and all of the lovely enzymes in that grain. This is very important to think about.

LIVE FOODS

Mae West was once my patient and followed many of my suggestions in her dieting program. One time on the stage, she said, "You know, I'm not interested in the men in my life, I'm interested in the life in my men." With this thought in mind, I think we should be interested in the life in our foods. The life in our vegetables is so powerfully influenced by the sunshine, that juice is called "liquid sunshine" many times. Life is enhanced by the air we breathe, the soil that feeds the plants we eat, and the water that carries the life-giving nutrients throughout each plant.

Soluble mineral elements are highly electrified and highly empowered by the activities of nature—fire, water, heat, air, oxygen and sunshine. These are the true properties that heal. Man cannot get away from those and cannot be well without them. This is the most important story you'll ever get in your life. If you want to see that you have the greatest amount of health, juice the live foods.

WHAT DO YOU NEED TO TAKE UP JUICING?

You should have a juicer. You should have a liquefier. You should work close to the chemical elements in live foods. But I want you to remember one thing. When you start eating an apple, by the time you get around to where you started on that apple, you will find that all that nice, white inner meat has turned brown. It has become oxidized. It's become oxidized in less than 2 minutes, sometimes less than that, if you'll just watch that white. The white of an apple turns brown when oxygen has come in and broken it down.

The values of having a juicer and a liquefier are to prepare these foods and have it ready *right now!* You are oxidizing those foods. They're going to spoil quickly. You leave orange juice out overnight, the next morning 15% of the vitamin C has been destroyed. It's gone! It goes back to the dust of the earth where it came from to begin with. This is the story we have to realize that we're in a world of change. There's nothing permanent in life but change. When we use fresh, live, juices and chemicals are coming and going; chemicals come to you in a live, electromagnetic form, given to you by natural processes, nature's way of replenishing the human body.

When you see a ripe berry, pick it and eat it. Don't save it for a week. It'll never do you any good. It's too late. Never pick a berry that is green. You know it is sour. It'll turn to a sour compound in your body. You must take it right on the button. And that's why they say in Boston they've never tasted a ripe blackberry. Why? Because they don't get it ripe!

When string beans are picked off the vine, they're alkaline-forming. In six days of storage they become acid-forming. You see very well what it means and why it's important to drink juice right after making it. We should get it to the digestive juices before any oxidation has taken place. That's where healing begins. And if you can see where this healing begins through perseverance, having this day in and day out, you'll finally remold, revitalize, remake and refurnish the body, refurbish the body and produce a new cell structure you can call a vital integrity that we need in the makeup of every cell in our body.

And, remember, in a closing remark here that we reach every cell in our body through the blood and through lymph derived from the blood, and through the soluble bio-chemicals that are life-giving. That's why it is so important to make fresh juices and juice combinations three or more times per day.

This is the story of the role juices have played in my life. This is the story we should look forward to, and get away from the idea of trying to cure a disease. Let us make a healthy body, chemically complete, fit for tomorrow and ready to meet any of the challenges of our life.

CHAPTER TWO

STARTING OUT WITH JUICES

Fresh juices, fruit and vegetable, can often add such a valuable nutritional boost to our regular diet that we notice a wonderful difference in how we feel after only a month or two. And, in a year's time of regular daily use of a variety of fresh juices, who knows that can happen? Relief from long-standing chronic disease is the reward of many who decide to change to a healthy diet and lifestyle—and stick with it!

I believe juices should be a regular part of everyone's daily food regimen. And, with the availability of wonderful, moderately-priced juicers, anyone can become an expert in juicing.

In days gone by, grandpa and grandma drank apple juice fresh from big, manually-operated apple presses. Grandma, if she lived in a region where citrus wasn't too expensive, made hand-squeezed orange juice by pushing cut orange halves back and forth over a small fluted dome in the middle of a shallow dish that caught and held the juice and pulp until there was enough to pour in a glass. Sometimes grape juice was made by mashing grapes in a colander and collecting the juice in a bowl below it, then putting the grape pulp in a clean flour sack to drip into the juice bowl until the last drop was gathered. In those days, I believe juice was more highly regarded than it is now because it was harder to come by and required more work. But, now that we know how much benefit we derive from juices, we should be eager to take advantage of the opportunity to live healthier, more energetic lives by making fresh juices a regular part of our lifestyle.

A NOTE OF CAUTION

On one hand, I'm pleased to see so many different juices and juice combinations and juice cocktails on the supermarket shelves—not to mention all the frozen juices ready to thaw, dilute and make up as soon as you get home. *But, these are not fresh juices, and they don't have the nutritional value of fresh juices.* If it was made last week or last year, what's fresh about it?

I'm suggesting that you beware of juices in bottles, cans or cartons. Such juices may be made either from fruit concentrates or imported fruits from countries that still use pesticides banned in the U.S., like DDT and others known to increase cancer risk. Or, they may be grown on soil depleted of important nutrients, which means that the fruit juice will lack nutrients. I'm not saying that all bottled, canned or cartoned juices are contaminated or terribly inferior. I'm saying they are seldom, if ever, as tasty or nutritionally potent as fresh juices. And, they may contain artificial chemical additives. Many times juices are diluted with water.

What's wrong with chemical additives? Basically, they are not natural to the body and they have to be detoxified, broken down and eliminated from the body just like any other foreign substance taken in. This robs the body of energy, ties up an unknown portion of immune system defenses and may contribute to liver damage. If there ever was such a thing as a "harmless" food additive, it could still become a carcinogen or poison by combining with another chemical or drug residue present in the system. I don't know about you, but I'd rather not take the chance. I prefer my foods—including juices—to be **whole, pure, natural and fresh!**

SIMPLY STARTING AND STARTING SIMPLY

It doesn't take much to get started in juicing single fruits or vegetables. You just buy a juicer and get going.

Shop around and find out what kinds of juicers are available. You'll find that there are still hand-operated juicers that work well with citrus fruits but not much else. I don't advise buying one because I believe most people use too much citrus and use too little of the many other juices available. So, live a little and sample some of the wonderful variety of juices from the many fruits in God's garden.

Look into electric juicers and find one in your price range that fits your needs. You might want to check in the consumers' guide books in your local library to see what they have to say about the comparative merits of the different juicers, and which ones are the best buys for the money.

You also need to learn how to pick out good fruits and vegetables for juicing, and I'll cover that in a later chapter. You should know that unsprayed, organically-raised fruits and vegetables are the best buys, best for your health.

After you've made some of the "single fruit" juices, you'll be ready to think about combining flavors and nutrients by mixing juices, or by adding other supplements to them in a blender.

JUICERS AND BLENDERS—A BIG DIFFERENCE

Juicers and blenders are made to do very different tasks. Most juicers have only one speed, while blenders have many speeds, but that's not the essential difference. The main difference is that juicers grind fruits and vegetables to pulp, then extract the juice from the pulp for you. Blenders either liquefy what is put in them or cut it into fine pieces. In other words, the pulp and juice are mixed together in one somewhat mushy mass.

Of course, you can extract juice with your juicer and combine the juice with other ingredients in a blender, to make some delicious and very nourishing combinations. For example, you can juice equal amounts of carrots and celery to make a lovely combination. Pour this juice into a blender (about a pint, for example), then add 1/4 cup of raw sunflower seeds that you've soaked overnight in pineapple juice, and blend until the seeds are well liquefied. The taste will surprise and please you, and this combination is not only rich in vitamin A, bio-organic sodium and calcium, but lecithin, vitamin E, fatty acids, zinc and many wonderful enzymes. It's a great health builder for the glands.

If you don't have a blender, I encourage you to get one. If you can only get one new appliance at this time, however, buy the juicer first and the blender later. I plan on including a whole chapter on blender drinks later in the book.

SOME FACTS OF LIFE ABOUT JUICERS

You can get a good centrifugal juicer that will juice "hard vegetables" like carrots, celery, beets, etc., by grinding them up on a spinning grinder plate, then throwing the pulp against the side of a spinning screen to separate the juice. Centrifugal juicers come with features of holding the pulp or spitting the pulp out an exit opening.

There are internal screw-type juicers that crush the fruits or vegetables pressed into them, then force the juice out by pressing the pulp against a heavy-duty, stainless-steel screen. This type of juicer also comes with a hydraulic press. One of the big advantages is that you can also use the screw-type juicer to make seed-or nut-butters. Both personal and heavy-duty commercial grade screw-type juicers are available.

Both the centrifugal and screw-type juicers clog up easily with soft fruit pulp or the pulp produced by running spinach or parsley through. If you want to run spinach or parsley through a juicer the right way, work them into the rotating screw inside the machine by forcing them in with carrots or celery. You will get a mixed juice, but enriched by the chlorophyll-rich juice of the spinach or parsley.

Wheat grass juice, if you've ever encountered it in a health food store, is possibly the most expensive juice on the market. Made famous by the Hippocrates Institute in Florida, wheat grass juice is simply the green, chlorophyll-rich juice of young blades of wheat grass. Some people grow their own wheat grass in a window box or a plot in the garden. This grass is ground to pulp in a special type of heavy-duty juicer, a slow-turning juicer. The slower turning of the blade inside the juicer housing pulps the wheat grass without causing oxidation, and removes the green juice. High-speed juicers don't seem to handle spinach, grass and other leaf-type green vegetables well at all. The green juices are used more for cleansing and may be the most appropriate juices for taking care of degenerative diseases.

WHY YOU SHOULD GET ON THE JUICE WAGON

We live in an age when hospital costs, doctors' fees and many medical services are so high, and disease statistics are so discouraging and overwhelming, that it makes good sense to protect yourself as much as you can from diseases and other health disturbances that occur so often.

Many modern diseases are linked with nutrient deficiencies by investigative research. Years of mineral deficiencies, for example, through poor or imbalanced food regimens, invite, encourage and sustain chronic diseases. Fresh juices help prevent nutrient deficiencies.

How can diet-related deficiencies cause diseases? All body cells are programmed to use internal energy and externally provided nutrients (through the blood and lymph) to do their jobs in the body. But, how can a cell do its job if it doesn't have the right kind of minerals to make the structure work right, or to form the protein it was designed to make?

The answer is, it can't. Once a cell becomes weakened by mineral deficiencies (usually multiple), it becomes a pushover for various processes that may lead to DNA-breakage in the cell nucleus, or to some other unfortunate malfunction. These breakdowns usually take place in the constitutionally weak parts of the body, where only a slight malfunction can have terrible consequences, such as the initiation of degenerative diseases, including asthma, kidney failure, emphysema, cancer or cardiovascular disease.

Juices, fresh and brimful of life, are an effective preventive measure and antidote for all health problems beginning with nutrient deficiencies. Juices have exactly the right ingredients for preventing or helping reverse disease.

CHAPTER THREE

GREENS IN YOUR JUICER

One of the great advantages of chlorophyll-rich juices is their cleansing effect on the bowel and other elimination systems, which results in a cleansing of the bloodstream and lymph system. A clean body is an efficient body, a body that digests well, assimilates well, and is full of energy and vigor. Sickness and disease seldom bother a clean body, or they leave when cleanliness is restored.

In the Introduction to this book, I introduced you to the healing power of green vegetable juice by describing my experience with the lady who had 13 leg ulcers. After doctors in two prestigious clinics were unable to help her, "Dr. Chlorophyll" showed her that nature cures. When we begin to juice greens, we touch on the cleansing aspect of healing, a seldom discussed issue these days.

REMEDIAL EFFECTS OF CHLOROPHYLL

- Builds a high blood count
- Counteracts toxins
- Helps purify the liver
- Feeds heart tissues iron
- Improves blood sugar problems
- Improves milk production
- Eliminates body odors
- Improves nasal drainage
- Relieves sore throat
- Soothes ulcer tissues
- Aids catarrhal discharges
- Improves varicose veins
- Provides iron to organs
- Cleans and deodorizes bowel
- Aids hepatitis
- Aids hemophilia
- Aids asthma
- Helps sores heal faster
- Destroys bacteria in wounds
- Slows nasal drip
- Benefits inflamed tonsils
- Soothes painful hemorrhoids
- Revitalizes vascular system in legs
- Reduces pain caused by inflammation

There are several types of greens you may use in juicing, and I want to turn aside to the subject of how we juice greens for a moment before we continue with the topic of cleansing.

JUICING WITH GRASSES AND HERBS

I have seen many patients helped with green juices, which contain chlorophyll, enzymes, iron, magnesium, phosphorus, potassium and sodium, as well as pro-vitamin A, vitamins B-Complex, C, E and K. The power of sunshine in chlorophyll is wonderfully cleansing in the body.

Potassium salts rich in the green juices, are supportive of heart function and neutralize muscle acids. Greens help protect the liver and gallbladder from the harmful effects of fats. The chlorophyll in greens cleanses the bowel and the bloodstream, and the pro-vitamin A (carotene) is said to be anti-carcinogenic, protective against cancer.

Greens are very high in this anti-cancer vitamin, but so are carrots. One of my patients at the Ranch some years ago lived on nothing but carrot juice for over a year. He had been diagnosed by his doctor as having a degenerative disease, and I could hardly believe what was passing from his bowel while he was on this carrot juice fast. In time, all his symptoms disappeared. Carrot juice is universally accepted by most people, while green juice from wheat grass, barley grass, alfalfa or green, leafy vegetables must either be diluted with water or some milder juice or else sipped very slowly. Green juice is very potent, and most people have to be careful with it.

GREEN JUICE AND DEGENERATIVE DISEASE

Ann Wigmore, founder of the Hippocrates Health Institute, is the one who has made raw wheat grass juice famous. She is a wonderful person, and I have the greatest respect for her work. She has demonstrated that the nutritional effects of "live" raw foods and juices are often accompanied by a powerful reversal of disease and restoration of energy in those who have come to her institute for help.

H.E. Kirschner, M.D., was another strong believer in the value of green juice. In the 1930s, Dr. Kirschner confirmed the healing value of green juice when he was in charge of 200 tuberculosis patients at the Olive View Sanitorium near Los Angeles. He gave these patients a "green drink" daily containing pineapple juice, alfalfa, parsley, mint, spinach, herbs, dried kelp powder, almonds, dates and sunflower seeds, all liquefied together in a blender. This drink was given as a supplement to their regular diet. Many patients gained weight, reported improved digestion and bowel function, and showed an increase in hemoglobin. Patients considered hopeless were out of bed in six to eight months.

I met Dr. Kirschner when he came out to my Ranch to interview a patient whose cancer symptoms disappeared after a lengthy juice fast. We shared much in common, both believing that nature cure and drugless healing were the best approach to true restoration of tissue integrity.

Here is his "green drink": Soak overnight in water 15 almonds, 4 pitted dates and 5 teaspoons full of sunflower seeds. In the morning, put these in a blender with pre-sweetened pineapple juice and blend thoroughly. Then, take 4 large handsful of greens (no stems), such as alfalfa, parsley, mint, spinach, beet greens, watercress, kale, chard, and herbs like filaree, malva, lamb's quarter and dandelion. Liquefy the greens in pineapple juice, then mix in the liquefied nuts, dates and seeds and liquefy together. Doesn't this sound good?

Now, Dr. Kirschner's "green drink" was not a juice drink but a blenderized drink. Nevertheless, you can make a wonderful green juice drink using the same principles, and here is how.

Basic green juice. You may use wheat grass, barley grass or alfalfa, but dilute with fresh parsley, mint, spinach or even celery. Flavor with pineapple or apple juice, if you wish, or dilute with distilled water. To this basic fresh, raw juice, you may add herbs—by juicing the fresh leaves, flowers or roots, by adding the dried powder to the juice and mixing, or by making an herbal tea first, then mixing it with the basic "green juice."

HERBAL TEAS DILUTED WITH JUICE

For a cooling summer drink for my patients and students, we often make up a big cooler of herbal tea mixed with juice.

Herbal teas with distinctive pleasant flavors like lemon grass tea or alfalfa-peppermint tea go well with apple juice, while other herbal teas go well with pineapple or blends of different fruits.

If you need an energy pickup, take a glass of any fruit or vegetable juice, add a heaping tablespoon of honeybee pollen, blenderize it for 30 seconds on high, and enjoy yourself. It tastes great and does good things for your energy.

MORE JUICE IDEAS AND THOUGHTS

When I was in Switzerland at the Bircher-Benner Institute, I watched them give beets to laboratory rats to reduce the rate of cancer growth. Beets are good for the liver, gallbladder and bowel, and I always try to include a little beet juice or grated beet (the size of a golf ball) in my food regimen every day. I have had bowel troubles off and on all my life, and I give great credit to beets and beet juice for keeping me on the go.

I remember when Dr. Garnett Cheney at Stanford University discovered that raw green cabbage juice can heal stomach ulcers. Juice half a head of green cabbage at a time and drink about a quart over the course of a day. You can flavor the cabbage juice with celery juice or pineapple if you can't take it as it is. Some people find the cabbage juice a little too potent for their taste, and prefer to take it diluted.

In many cases of bleeding bowel, I have suggested that patients use green juice or liquid chlorophyll in their enema water. Chlorophyll has a soothing, cleansing, healing influence on the bowel.

Many years ago, I had a lady come to the Ranch who had a very limited, delicate constitution due to over a hundred diverticula along one side of her colon. Her doctor wanted to cut out that section of her colon, but she came all the way to my California Ranch from back East, looking for an alternative.

Almost all foods upset her digestion. I found out that one thing she tolerated very well was goat milk, so I put this patient on a goat milk diet. Milk, however, lacks iron, so we had to add a little green juice to the milk to make sure she wouldn't get anemic. This lady stayed with me on the Ranch for over 30 years, working as an employee. I've never had a harder-working employee, even though all she had in her diet was goat milk and chlorophyll or green juice.

ANOTHER WAY TO JUICE

If you can't afford to buy a juicer (you should be able to save up for one), you can make wheat grass or barley grass juice or juice from any other combination of greens by putting distilled water in a blender, adding handsful of greens and letting the blender chop them very fine. Pour into a crock or other large container and let soak in a cool area two hours. Then strain out the solids by using cheesecloth or some other kind of cloth, and you'll have your green drink—diluted, but still fresh and powerful.

DR. JENSEN'S DRINK

When I get tired or feel the need for an energy pickup, I ask for my drink. My friends and employees just call it, "Doctor Jensen's Drink." The base is either goat milk or soy milk (made with soy powder **not** soy flour), and this is mixed half-and-half with carrot juice or green juice. A teaspoon of almond butter or sesame seed butter is added, then a teaspoon of some natural sweetener, like honey, maple sugar or date sugar. On occasion, I ask for a sliver of avocado, a half banana or a little beet juice to be added. And, this is my drink.

You're welcome to try it. Perhaps you'll add a touch of your own to increase your own enjoyment, or add a particular nutrient that you know you need. That's the fun of juicing and making up blender drinks.

You can get as creative as you want!

It is possible to purchase special slow-grinding juicers called wheat grass juicers, which press the juice from barley grass, wheat grass, alfalfa, sprouts and other greens. But you can also juice greens in a fast screw-type juicer, if you juice them together with a "hard" vegetable like carrots or celery. The hard vegetables give bulk or body to the soft greens, which give up their juice along with that of the harder vegetable.

This process of mixing hinders you from getting a pure green juice, but you will find the pure green juice so powerful that you will want to dilute it. Remember, I didn't have a juicer when the lady with the 13 leg ulcers came to me. I had her cut up all the leafy vegetables by hand, but the juice from them was diluted by distilled water. That made it mild and easy to drink.

HOW TO GROW WHEAT GRASS

Wheat grass not only contains an abundance of pro-vitamin A and chlorophyll, it is rich in minerals and enzymes. It contains protein, prostaglandins and trace elements. Because of its high nutritional value, some people like to grow it at home.

To grow wheat grass, soak wheat berries in water overnight, and plant them the next morning in a tray or window box with at least an inch of moist dirt. Don't worry about making it deeper, because you are going to harvest the wheat grass before it gets very high. Sprinkle the whole wheat berries on top of the soil in the box and sprinkle dirt on top of them until they are covered about 1/4" deep. Water lightly each day, just enough to keep the soil damp. When the grass is 5 or 6 inches tall, cut it low and make juice out of it.

The pulp from wheat grass makes a wonderful poultice for drawing out the toxins in wounds, infections, boils and cysts. Place the pulp over the desired spot, cover with a moist cloth, then cover the most cloth with a dry cloth or towel.

Of course, you can buy liquid chlorophyll made from alfalfa in most health food stores. It's good but it isn't fresh. Fresh green juice contains live enzymes, as do all raw foods, and those enzymes are the spark plugs that energize the hundreds of thousands of chemical reactions that go on in the body every moment, tearing down, building up and changing one thing to another. An enzyme is a complex, active protein that is able to trigger a change in another substance without being changed itself. The more enzymes we take in with juices and foods, the less energy our own bodies have to spend in processing and using our foods as they are broken down into elementary particles.

If you can't get your juicer to process greens, and you want to juice them, you might put them in a blender with distilled water, then strain the debris out through cheesecloth. It will be diluted, of course, but that's not bad. Diluted green juices are easier to take. Not everyone can afford two or more juicers.

Freshly prepared green juices are sometimes used in programs to reverse chronic or degenerative diseases. Do they work? Along with a balanced diet, I would say they help a great deal.

WHAT'S IN A GREEN JUICE?

When I talk about "green juice," I'm covering a lot of territory. This includes dandelion greens, collard greens, mustard greens, beet greens, kale, spinach, chard, sprouts of many kinds, alfalfa, wheat grass, barley grass, turnip greens, watercress, parsley, cabbage and asparagus. Green juices have many good things in common.

First of all, let's understand chlorophyll. Chlorophyll in the leaves of plants is a chemical powerhouse activated by sunlight to draw carbon dioxide from the air through the pores of the leaves. By splitting water molecules apart and recombining their hydrogen and oxygen with the carbon and oxygen of the carbon dioxide, carbohydrates are formed. All this takes place in the presence of chlorophyll. Carbohydrates are plant sugars or starches, some of which are stored in the roots of fruit of the plant, along with vitamins, minerals, enzymes, a little oil, a little protein and a lot of water.

Chlorophyll is often called the "life blood" of plants, and the basic chlorophyll molecule is nearly identical to the hemoglobin molecule of the blood. The main difference is that there is an iron molecule in the center of the hemoglobin structure, while there is a magnesium molecule in the center of the chlorophyll molecule. Surprisingly, most green vegetables contain a milligram or two of iron per 100-gram portion, in addition to the magnesium from the chlorophyll. Just to give you some idea of the quantity involved in a couple of different vegetables, 100 grams of raw parsley contains 6.2 mg of iron and 41 mg of magnesium, while 100 gm of watercress contains 1.7 mg of iron and 18.6 mg of magnesium. We need an average total intake of 18 mg of iron daily.

THE SECRET OF MY WORK

The secret of my work is building a high blood count in my patients, and nothing does better at building a good red blood cell count than green vegetable juices. A high red blood cell count means that more oxygen can be delivered to the tissues to aid in cellular respiration.

A third-generation vegetarian from Canada brought his daughter to me for help in correcting an anemic condition. She was a fourth-generation vegetarian, and had refused to take any animal-derived supplements. I gave her eight chlorophyll-rich drinks daily, and her red blood count rose from 2,800,000 to 3,800,000 in a month's time. When she left the Ranch, her blood count was 4,500,000, almost normal.

She regained her health and became very active and vigorous. She is married now, and her children are healthy and strong.

Vitamin K, the blood-clotting factor, is a fat-soluble vitamin found in all greens, an additional benefit. Vitamin A, in the form of carotene, is rich in all green vegetables as well as in carrot juice. Science has found out that a diet high in carotene lowers the risk of cancer. Greens range from 50 mg to 200 mg of calcium per 100-gm serving, and most are high in potassium. There's a trace of copper and zinc in most greens.

Juice made from greens helps control calcium in the body, which assists in healing. It feeds the desirable bacteria and cleanses the bowel. It increases the blood-clotting ability as it builds up and cleanses the bloodstream. Experiments earlier in this century show that chlorophyll has antiseptic properties and is effective in disinfecting wounds. It is also a rejuvenating factor when used with a balanced diet. We find out that green juices are a special gift from mother nature in detoxifying, cleansing and restoring a polluted, rundown body. (Refer to Dr. Jensen's book *The Healing Power of Chlorophyll*.)

SETTLING ON A RIGHT PROGRAM FOR LIVING

I want to point out that it isn't enough to drink a few glasses of fresh juice daily, hoping to compensate for poor eating habits and an unhealthy lifestyle. If you want to live a long, healthy life, you will have to take a new path in life, and juices are only a small—though important—part of that new path.

A balanced diet, such as my Health and Harmony Food Regimen, is essential to a right way of living. Juices and other food supplements are used to "fine tune" the diet to meet your individual needs. Regular exercise is another absolute necessity, along with adequate sleep and rest, and plenty of fresh air.

I love juices and what they do for my health, but I wouldn't have the health I possess at the age of 84 (as of this writing), if I hadn't followed a total health program, a path of right living.

FRIENDS FROM THE GARDEN AND FIELD

The following is a list of the finest green plants and vegetables for juicing that I know. Variety is a key to better health, so change the greens you use for juicing every few days or so.

ALFALFA. I recommend the use of fresh alfalfa in the basic green juice, not just as an additive, if you can get it fresh. Alfalfa is very deep-rooted, picking up trace elements, as well as the calcium, magnesium, phosphorus, iron and potassium, for which it is well-known.

Use it for purifying the blood and digestive problems. Helps arthritis (use with chaparral), allergies, morning sickness and the endocrine glands.

Alfalfa in the form of sprouts is one of the purest foods we can have for the body. Sprouts promote healthy bowel activity. Alfalfa tablets are helpful in keeping bowel pockets and other areas free of stagnant putrefactive materials. The alfalfa teas are excellent sources of alkalinity.

ANISE. This aromatic herb is often available in markets and health food stores in season and may be growing wild near your home. A little fresh anise in your green juice will reduce or eliminate gas formation in the stomach and bowel.

BEET GREENS. Beet greens, containing potassium, magnesium, iodine and iron, are an excellent body mineralizer. Clean and wash thoroughly. Use stems if they are tender. Beet greens juice is wonderful for the liver and gallbladder. A half glass per day will also help bowel movements.

BOK CHOY. This Chinese cabbage is high in sulfur and iron, and is also high in potassium. Sulfur purifies and activates the body and tones the system.

BRUSSELS SPROUTS. This member of the cabbage family is also high in sulfur. Many people find it gas-forming in a raw juice, so be cautious.

CABBAGE. Cabbage juice is excellent for the stomach. It contains sodium, the youth element, which is stored there and also potassium, the muscle toner. A medical doctor at Stanford cleared up ulcers of the stomach using cabbage juice as a remedy. Use raw cabbage in salads. There is more vitamin C in a half cup of raw cabbage than in a medium-sized orange.

CAYENNE. I recommend adding a little powdered cayenne right in the juicer, no more than 1/2 tsp at first, for the circulation. Cayenne is good for the heart and blood pressure, for asthma and upper respiratory conditions, to boost energy and endurance. You can use it with raw garlic (one or two buttons) to help lower blood pressure.

CELERY GREENS. Celery greens should be juiced along with the stalk. The potassium in the green tops balances the high sodium content of the stalk. If a person just takes the stalk, he will be getting a concentrated form of sodium. The overabundance of sodium causes water to be held in the body. An overabundance of potassium can also cause problems, but few people ever get too much potassium because our body requires so much of it. It specifically feeds the muscle structure which makes up 80% of our body.

CHAPARRAL. Like alfalfa, chaparral is a good blood cleanser and is especially effective juiced with other greens, providing a high-chlorophyll tonic to sweeten and cleanse the bowel. Chaparral is used most often for arthritis and degenerative conditions in the body.

CHIVES. These are high in potassium, calcium and sulfur. Chives are good for catarrhal elimination.

CORIANDER (CILANTRO). This wonderful culinary herb improves the taste of soups, salads, meat, fish and poultry, and it also strengthens the heart and acts as a tonic to the digestive system. Juice a handful of fresh, green coriander in your green drink for a special list.

DANDELION. Use the leaves and root if you want to cleanse the kidneys, liver and gallbladder. This herb is also good for the bowel, spleen and pancreas. Good for anemia, diabetes, hypoglycemia, low blood pressure and skin troubles. Mild diuretic. These greens are fine sources of calcium, manganese, chlorine, potassium and iron.

ECHINACEA. This herb is a powerful detoxifying agent, and I recommend that it be made into a tea first by simmering in water for 8 to 10 minutes, before adding to juice and mixing thoroughly. Purchase echinacea at a health food store and follow directions on container concerning suggested amount to add. This is one of the best cleansers for the lymph system, and has given good results in some cases of degenerative disease.

ENDIVE. While endive is bitter, it is also excellent for reducing. Wash before juicing.

ESCAROLE. Here is another lettuce family member which is high in potassium. Add fruit juice to make it more palatable.

GREEN KALE. Here is one of the highest greens in calcium. It also belongs to the sulfur family.

MALVA. This wild weed grows heavily throughout the United States and elsewhere. One pound has 50,000 units of natural vitamin A which is so important in clearing up infections. Malva is tasty in salads and can be steamed like spinach. Be sure to clean the leaves first, using a teaspoon of Purex to a gallon of water. Soak the leaves for five minutes and then wash them off.

NASTURTIUM FLOWERS. These make another source of greens. Have them in salads too.

PARSLEY. Parsley makes an outstanding chlorophyll drink for the kidneys. You can dry it and make a parsley tea. Always use in soup and broth. There is more iron in parsley than any other herb I know. It is high in pro-vitamin A, a natural anticarcinogenic, and in chlorophyll, nature's most powerful cleanser. Parsley is often available all Winter long in the fresh vegetable department at your local market. Use it generously in your green juice.

Parsley helps with kidney and gallstones, cleanses the liver, supports the heart and is a good tonic for the blood vessels. Some report that it has helped their arthritis (all green herbs and leafy vegetables help reduce symptoms of arthritis, but some better than others). Parsley is one of the few herbs that helps deodorize garlic or onion breath.

PEPPERMINT, SPEARMINT, MINT. These herbs are high in chlorophyll. They make excellent flavorings for bitter drinks. They are wonderful when it comes to driving gas out of the intestinal tract and they also make the tract smell sweet.

SAGE. A potent herb that I used to point out to my patients at the Ranch on our morning walks. I'd tell them to pick some, rub it in their hands and smell it. Sage will open your eyes, your sinuses and wake up a sleepy head right away.

We find that a little sage added to your green drink will decrease secretions of the mucous membranes, help with digestive and bowel problems, reduce nervousness and night sweats, expel parasites from the bowel, reduce morning sickness and nausea and help with skin problems. It is well to know that sage may act as a sexual depressant in some persons.

SPINACH. Try to have a little bit in a raw juice but do not overdo it because it contains oxalic acid which interferes with the absorption of calcium in the body. Swiss chard and beet greens also contain this acid—so does chocolate. Considering the wide variety of greens in the garden, spinach should be eaten about once a week.

SWISS CHARD. A brother of the spinach, this family member is a little more palatable than its kin. It also contains oxalic acid.

THYME. This popular cooking herb not only enhances flavor in foods but is a strong stimulant for catarrhal elimination from the upper respiratory system and an effective headache remedy. It reduces the symptoms of asthma and hay fever, helps digestion, reduces flu discomfort and sore throat, and may help prevent kidney stones.

TURNIP GREENS. I have referred to Dr. Goldstein's contribution to health of the South when he recommended using these greens to control calcium metabolism in the body. When Dr. Goldstein used this remedy, most symptoms of pellagra disappeared.

WATERCRESS. This is one of the greatest of our garden friends for trimming off excess weight. Anyone overweight should consider getting more potassium and less sodium in the diet. This is a high potassium food. Sodium holds water while potassium helps get rid of it. Because it grows along streams, it is seldom sprayed.

WHEAT GRASS JUICE. This is one of the finest health builders I know.

Fresh herbs are not as potent as the dried, powdered form; or herbal teas, decoctions or extracts (alcohol-dissolved herbal essences); but they are, like other "live" nutrients, nature's potentized and triturated remedies—whole, pure and natural—and their fresh juice adds the special healing touch found only in herbs.

For a special taste treat, add fresh lemon grass, spearmint or peppermint or licorice to green juice sweetened with fresh, natural pineapple juice.

Herbs commonly found fresh at the supermarket these days (in season) include coriander, parsley, lemon grass, tarragon, mint, sage, marjoram, rosemary, oregano, thyme, basil, anise, garlic and chives. Some of these are primarily used in cooking, while others have distinctive healing value as well. I advise you to get my new book *HERBS: WONDER HEALERS,* so you can increase the healing power of your fresh juices even more.

This list is by no means complete, but is intended as a reminder of some of the valuable foods we have in the garden. I hope you begin using them, if you are not already doing so.

CHAPTER FOUR

BEST FRUITS AND VEGETABLES
FOR JUICING

I believe we should use juices according to season, just as
we use the full fruits and vegetables according to season, with
some common sense deviations. Where winters are cold, and ice
and snow rule out any homegrown fruit or vegetables, you may
use what you find available in the stores, or reconstitute dried
fruit by soaking overnight, starting with boiling water. I urge
you, however, to follow nature's law of variety in foods by also
using a variety of juices. Don't just have the same juice or juice
combination every day.

Variety in what we eat and drink is the only real "insurance"
we can get to make sure our bodies are getting all the chemical
elements and nutrients we need.

Because vitamin B-12 is so necessary, yet so lacking in fruits
and vegetables, I advise adding a couple of grams of chlorella
to your juice twice a day, blending in your blender. Chlorella is
very high in vitamin B-12, as well as in the nucleic factors that
help us stay young and in a growth factor that stimulates
healing. You can't go wrong in making this addition. Chlorella
is available in most health food stores.

Vegetables keep longer because they have lower sugar and
moisture content. For the same reason, many of the soft
fruits—if they are fully ripe—are almost as quickly and easily
digested and assimilated as fruit juices. It is harder to juice soft
fruits, however, because the soft pulp keeps clogging the
straining portion of the juicers. For this reason, some soft fruits
are better processed into "nectars," such as peach or apricot.

*All juices should be used within six hours after they are
made, but preferably within one hour.*

In my book *Foods That Heal*, I have a complete guide of fruits and vegetables. I have spent many years collecting the information that appears in this guide. I hope the information will be valuable to you. This guide to foods that heal shows how to use foods as medicine, in the tradition of V.G. Rocine and Hippocrates.

Each fruit or vegetable is described in considerable detail, and the therapeutic value of the food is given. Not every fruit or vegetable is in this guide. I have only included the ones for which I could get all the information I wanted to share with you. Please refer to my book *Foods That Heal.*

ANALYTICAL FOOD GUIDE

On the following pages, we have included our Analytical Food Guide for your assistance in selecting the fruits and vegetables for juicing and liquefying. This chart includes the food and type, predominant chemical elements, the best way prepared and served for good digestion and the remedial measures.

This chart will aid your selection of foods for any particular health requirements. We hope you will find the information to be very helpful, as it has proven to be a valuable tool in our work for many years.

Food and Type	Predominant Chemical Elements	Best Way Prepared and Served For Digestion	Remedial Measures
Almond Nuts Protein Fat	Manganese Phosphorus Potassium	Serve with vegetables or fruits. Almonds, celery, and apple: a complete meal. Make almond nut milk drink.	Muscle, brain and nerve food. Best of nuts to use.
Apples Mineral	Potassium Sodium Magnesium	Wash, eat alone, in salads or with proteins. Give to children in between meals, Juice or liquefy them.	Apple skins used for tea. Fine for kidney and urinary tract. Good bowel and liver regulators.
Apricots Mineral	Potassium Phosphorus Iron Silicon Copper	Use only fresh or dried (unsulphured), alone, with whipped cream, or in salads. Make into apricot whip, add flaked nuts. Juice or liquefy them.	Good for anemia, constipation and catarrh.
Artichokes Mineral	Iodine Potassium Iron Silicon	Wash and steam. Use as cooked vegetable.	Good for soft bulk and minerals and as general body builder.
Asparagus Mineral	Calcium Iron Silicon Iodine	Cut tender portion from woody base. Remove scales if sandy. Cut up fine and steam. Juice or liquefy them.	Good for kidney and bladder disorders.
Avocado Mineral Fat	Chlorine Phosphorus Sulphur	Wash and peel. Eat alone, have in salads and soups. Good in sandwich filling. Goes well in any combination. Liquefy in any juice to make it a "smoothy."	Body builder. Good for colitis, ulcers. Use as natural oil and bulk in intestines. Slightly laxative and good mineralizer for the body.
Banana Carbohydrate	Potassium Calcium Chlorine	Buy when spotted and no green tops. Wash. Eat alone or in salads, serve as a starch. Eat dead-ripe or baked. ½ banana will make a more soothing drink.	Good for gaining weight. Used as natural bulk for irritated bowels, such as colitis, ulcers or diarrhea.

(Continued)

45

Food and Type	Predominant Chemical Elements	Best Way Prepared and Served For Digestion	Remedial Measures
Barley Carbohydrate Protein	Potassium Silicon	Use unpearled. Wash, steam and serve as a starch, alone or in soups. Juice can be added to barley group or soup.	For gaining weight. Excellent for children up to ten years for silicon content.
Bass Protein	Phosphorus Chlorine Iodine	Broil, bake or steam. Serve with natural sauces, or lemon.	Brain and nerve food. Use head, fins, and tail in broth for nerves and glands. Refer to Broths.
Beans, Lima Carbohydrate Protein	Potassium Phosphorus Calcium Iron	Shell and wash fresh limas, steam or use in vegetable and protein loaves. Cooked can be juiced and liquefied for many combinations.	Pureed for stomach ulcers. Good muscle-building food.
Beans, String Mineral	Manganese Nitrogen	Wash, remove ends and strings. Cut once lengthwise and cut crosswise in one-inch strips. Steam. Juice.	Good body mineralizer.
Beef Protein	Phosphorus Potassium Chlorine	Should be broiled or roasted. Serve with green vegetables and tomatoes or grapefruit.	Brain and nerve food. Good in anemia, for those over 20, and for those who use up surplus energies.
Beets Mineral Carbohydrate	Potassium Fluorine Chlorine	Cut off leaves, leaving one-inch stems. Steam. Also shred and steam for variation. Best juice for gallbladder and liver troubles and it is laxative in its effect.	Beet juice when combined with blackberry juice is a good blood builder. Use leaves like spinach.
Beet Greens Mineral	Potassium Magnesium Iodine Iron	Clean and wash thoroughly. Use stems if tender. Cut up fine and steam like spinach. Juice—have small amounts.	Body mineralizer.

(Continued)

Food and Type	Predominant Chemical Elements	Best Way Prepared and Served For Digestion	Remedial Measures
Blackberries Mineral	Potassium Magnesium Iodine Iron	Wash and serve alone, with other fruit, or with protein. What juices these berries make!	Blood builder. Used for dysentery or diarrhea. Good for anemia.
Blueberries Mineral	Potassium Calcium Magnesium	Wash and serve alone, with other fruit, or with protein. Juice and liquefy.	Blood purifier and body mineralizer.
Bread, Whole Wheat Protein Carbohydrate	Phosphorus Chlorine Calcium Silicon	To be eaten once a day with raw vegetable juices and salads. Sandwiches allowed but vegetable filling should be used.	When used discriminately, good for teeth, muscles, bones, and anemia.
Broccoli Mineral	Potassium	Remove tough leaves, tough part of stalk. Wash thoroughly and steam. Juice or liquefy.	Body mineralizer.
Butter, Cow Fat Mineral	Sodium Calcium Chlorine	Eaten on toast and served with vegetables in moderation. Use sweet butter.	Good for eyes; supplies Vitamin A, if not used in excess. Easiest fat to digest. Use on burns, skin inflammations.
Buttermilk Mineral Protein	Sodium Calcium Chlorine	Best with citrus fruit or protein. Juices can be added to this.	Good for diarrhea, gas, intestinal gas normalizer, and for acidity.
Brussels Sprouts	Potassium Calcium Sulphur	Remove wilted leaves. Leave whole. Wash and soak in salt water thirty minutes. Steam. Can liquefy.	Good mineralizer.

(Continued)

47

Food and Type	Predominant Chemical Elements	Best Way Prepared and Served For Digestion	Remedial Measures
Cabbage Mineral	Potassium Sodium	Remove wilted outside leaves. Cut in fourths. Wash, soak in salt water. Boil 7 minutes in uncovered pot. Use raw in salad. Juice is wonderful. Dr. Cheney says "cures ulcers of stomach".	Good mineralizer.
Carrots Mineral Carbohydrate	Potassium Calcium Sulphur Silicon	Clean with vegetable brush. Shred fine, use in salads, raw or steamed. A raw whole carrot daily develops children's teeth and jaws. High in beta carotene. Mildest of all juices. Mixes with any other juice.	Eye food. Good for hair, nails. Easy to digest. One of the best foods to break a fast. Shred finely.
Casaba Mineral	Potassium Sodium Chlorine Iron Silicon	Eat like other melons. Fill center with berries or sour cream. Good on hot afternoons. Juices you will never forget!	Blood cleanser and cooler.
Cauliflower Mineral	Potassium Calcium Sulphur Silicon	Remove leaves and woody base. Break flowers apart. Soak in salt water thirty minutes. Steam.	Good intestinal cleanser.
Celery Mineral	Chlorine Sodium Potassium Magnesium	Best eaten raw or in vegetable juice. May also be used steamed or in vegetable broth. High in sodium. For joints it is superb. Juice or liquefy.	For arthritis, neuritis, rheumatism, acidity, high blood pressure, and nerves. Juice form for good health; for every disease. Good blood cleanser.
Chayote Mineral	Potassium Magnesium Silicon	Wash, peel, cube, or slice and steam. Juice it—try it.	Non-fattening and a good mineralizer.

(Continued)

48

Food and Type	Predominant Chemical Elements	Best Way Prepared and Served For Digestion	Remedial Measures
Cheese, Cow Cottage Protein	Calcium Phosphorus Chlorine	Eaten as protein. Always serve with fruit and vegetables.	Hard to digest, but good source of complete protein. Dry or Farmer Style best.
Cheese, Goat Cottage Protein	Calcium Phosphorus Fluorine Chlorine	Always serve with fruit or vegetables.	Has fluorine in abundance. Good for bones, teeth, beauty, especially for children.
Cheese Roquefort Protein	Calcium Phosphorus Fluorine Chlorine	Always serve with fruit or vegetables.	Has fluorine in abundance. Good for bones and teeth.
Cheese Swiss Protein	Calcium Phosphorus Chlorine Sodium	Always serve with fruit or vegetables.	Good body builder.
Cherries, Wild Black Mineral	Potassium Iron Magnesium	Eat alone or serve with protein. High in iron. Juice or liquefy them.	For anemia, catarrh. Use one glass for three days in succession twice a month for chronic gallbladder trouble.
Chervil Mineral	Potassium Iron Phosphorus Sulphur	An herb eaten with salads, vegetables, proteins, or carbohydrates. Add a little juice to any other juice.	Body mineralizer.

(Continued)

Food and Type	Predominant Chemical Elements	Best Way Prepared and Served For Digestion	Remedial Measures
Chicken Protein	Phosphorus Potassium Chlorine	Serve with non-starch vegetables and tomatoes or grapefruit.	
Chicory Mineral	Iron Sulphur Chlorine Potassium	A green to be served in salad.	Body mineralizer.
Chinese Cabbage Mineral	Sodium Iron Calcium Magnesium	Serve raw in a salad, or prepared like cabbage.	Body mineralizer.
Chives Mineral	Potassium Calcium Sulphur	Served in salads, with vegetables, or in cottage cheese.	Body mineralizer, good for catarrh.
Coconuts Protein Fat Mineral	Potassium Magnesium Phosphorus Chlorine	Milk and coconut meat eaten with fresh or diced fruit or vegetables.	Body builder and for weight building. Good for bones and teeth.
Corn Carbohydrate Protein	Potassium Phosphorus Silicon	Remove husk and silks with a stiff brush. Steam. Eat with green vegetables. Yellow corn better than white corn.	A great brain, bone, and muscle-building food.
Cranberries Mineral	Calcium Sulphur Chlorine	Never eat. Too high in oxalic acid.	Use as pack in rectum for hemorrhoids.

(Continued)

50

Food and Type	Predominant Chemical Elements	Best Way Prepared and Served For Digestion	Remedial Measures
Cream, Cow Fat	Calcium Phosphorus Fluorine	Eat with fruit or vegetables.	Weight builder. Put on chapped or sunburned skin.
Cucumbers Mineral	Potassium Calcium Phosphorus Silicon Iron	Eaten in salad. Serve with a starch or protein. Best in summer drinks. Juice or liquefy.	Good for skin troubles, and for blood cooling.
Currants, Black Mineral	Phosphorus Magnesium Potassium	Used as a sweet, dried fruit; juice of fresh currants makes a refreshing drink. Try drinking them.	Blood builder.
Dandelion Greens Mineral	Potassium Calcium Manganese Chlorine	Discard greens with bud or blossoms as they are bitter. Cut off roots. Clean and wash thoroughly. Mix with sweet vegetables. Eat raw in salad or steam. Your liver would like this. Juice or liquefy.	Cleanses liver and gallbladder. Body mineralizer.
Dates, Dry Carbohydrate	Chlorine	Wash, eat alone, or with sub-acid fruits or vegetables. Candy substitute. Can sweeten some liquefied foods.	Good for undernourishment.
Duck Protein	Potassium Phosphorus Chlorine	Broil or roast. Serve with green vegetables and grapefruit or tomatoes.	An easy protein to digest.
Eggplant Mineral	Potassium Phosphorus Chlorine	With protein or starch as a vegetable. Wash, steam or bake whole, sliced, or cubed. May be stuffed or used in roasts and loaves. Can be juiced or liquefied.	Good form of bulk. Good mineralizer.

(Continued)

51

Food and Type	Predominant Chemical Elements	Best Way Prepared and Served For Digestion	Remedial Measures
Egg, Raw Protein **Egg Yolk** Mineral	Sulphur Chlorine Iodine Iron	Slowly cook, never fry, and serve with green vegetables, grapefruit, tomatoes or fruit. Egg drop soup ala Chinese. Put in any drink raw or soft boiled. Only good eggs should be used.	Excellent food for children. Brain, nerve, and gland food.
Endive Mineral	Potassium Calcium Sulphur	Wash and serve in salads. Juice it—mix with carrot juice.	Body mineralizer.
Figs, Black Carbohydrate	Potassium Magnesium	Wash and eat alone, or with fruits. Good candy substitute. Fig juice? Yes!	A natural laxative. Fig juice is a good drink when acid fruit juice cannot be taken.
Grapefruit, Fresh Mineral	Sodium Potassium Calcium	Eaten alone, or with fruit or protein. Buy grapefruit when it has a brownish yellow cast. Juice them.	For fevers and reducing. Blood cooling, and catarrh eliminator.
Grapes Mineral	Potassium Magnesium	Wash and serve alone or with other fruit or protein. Concord grapes are best. Juice seeds and all.	Blood purifier. Grape diet once or twice every year. Good for intestinal cleansing and all catarrhal conditions.
Halibut, Smoked Protein	Phosphorus Potassium Chlorine	Serve with green vegetables and grapefruit or tomatoes. Steam, bake or broil.	Good source of complete protein. Good source of brain and nerve fat.
Honey Carbohydrate	Potassium Calcium Phosphorus	Because it is a concentrated sweet, use sparingly with starches and green vegetables. Sweetening to taste.	Honey with onions makes good cough syrup—allow to stand overnight. Eucalyptus honey good for throat ailments. *(Continued)*

52

Food and Type	Predominant Chemical Elements	Best Way Prepared and Served For Digestion	Remedial Measures
Horseradish Mineral	Sulphur Fluorine Potassium	Used in seasoning salads, salad dressings, sandwich filling and sauces. Take some in juice—not too much.	Gallbladder and liver cleanser. Body mineralizer.
Kale Mineral	Calcium Potassium	With green vegetables in salad. Wash, cut fine and use raw or in soups. Highest in calcium. Juice it for bones, teeth and vitality. Don't overdo it.	Green kale broth for body calcium. Best source of calcium. Hardens teeth and bones. Body mineralizer.
Kohlrabi Mineral	Calcium Magnesium Potassium	Wash, peel, then cube, slice or shred, and steam. Can be juiced or liquefied.	Body mineralizer.
Lamb Protein	Potassium Phosphorus Chlorine	Bake or broil. Serve with green vegetables and tomatoes or grapefruit.	Good source of protein. Brain, gland, nerve food.
Leeks Mineral	Sodium Calcium	With green vegetables. Wash and use in salads. Put some in your juicer.	Good for catarrhal conditions. Body mineralizer.
Lemons Mineral	Calcium Magnesium Potassium	To be used alone as a drink or in salads served with a protein meal. Use instead of vinegar. Cuts sweetness of grape juice when added.	Catarrh elimination. Best used in fevers and liver disorders. Use in douches, enemas. High in lime salts. Blood cooler; weight reducer. Good germicidal agent. Skin bleach.
Lentils Protein Carbohydrate	Phosphorus Potassium	To be served with a green salad. Soak and cook until soft.	Muscle builder. Good when pureed for stomach ulcers and colitis.

(Continued)

53

Food and Type	Predominant Chemical Elements	Best Way Prepared and Served For Digestion	Remedial Measures
Lettuce, Head Mineral	Sodium Calcium Chlorine Potassium Iron	Wash well and use in salads. Green outside leaves are always best.	Slows up digestion. Good for sleeplessness. In severe gas conditions stop using in diet.
Lettuce, Romaine Mineral	Calcium Sodium Potassium Chlorine	With green vegetables, in raw salads, with starches or proteins. Leaf lettuce best. As juice, it's wonderful.	Mineralizer for the body.
Lettuce, Sea Mineral	Iodine Potassium Phosphorus Iron	Use powdered over salads, in drinks, or sprinkled on steamed vegetables.	Good source of iodine.
Limes Mineral	Calcium Magnesium Potassium	To be used in a drink or on salads served with a protein meal. Flavor it and change taste. Juice or liquefy.	Limes in whey, good as a blood cooler. Marvelous in congestion of the brain.
Mangoes Mineral	Potassium Calcium Chlorine	Eaten like melons or served in salads. Liquefy. A wonderful juice.	Good for irritated intestinal disorders.
Milk, Cow Protein	Calcium Sodium Phosphorus	To be served with fruits. Served as a protein. Add any vegetable juice to any milk product such as yogurt or kefir.	Complete protein. Use on eyes as a pack for inflammation.
Milk, Goat Protein	Sodium Fluorine Calcium Phosphorus	Use in place of cow milk. Always have raw. ½ goat milk and ½ carrot juice has been introduced to all my patients.	Better source of fluorine than cow milk. Easier digested than cow milk. Use raw. *(Continued)*

54

Food and Type	Predominant Chemical Elements		Best Way Prepared and Served For Digestion	Remedial Measures
Mushrooms Mineral	Potassium Phosphorus	Iodine	Used as flavoring in meat substitutes, roasts, and in sauces.	Body mineralizer.
Muskmelon Mineral	Sodium Potassium Silicon		Eat alone or with proteins, or cut up in salads with other fruit. Cantaloupe juice—it's a wow!	Good mineralizer, blood cooler. Use instead of artificial soft drink.
Mustard Greens Mineral	Sulphur Potassium Calcium Magnesium		Wash thoroughly, cut fine, and use in salads, or steam as a green vegetable. May be mixed with other greens. Have a little of these greens in your juice.	Good body mineralizer, or source of calcium. Good liver and gallbladder cleanser.
Oats, Steel Cut Mineral Carbohydrate	Silicon Iodine Magnesium		Use with green vegetables, or raw salad. Must be well cooked. Soak before cooking.	Excellent children's food, especially when they lack silicon. Good source of silicon.
Okra Mineral	Sodium Chlorine		Wash pods. Cut off stems. Use in broth and soups or steam. Serve separately with butter. High sodium food—try it in liquid form and mixed with other juices.	Good for stomach ulcers, irritated intestinal tract. Use in all broths for stomach disorders.
Olives Mineral Fat	Potassium Phosphorus		Serve with green vegetables, raw salad, or fruit. Throw in a few olives with your glass of juice.	Best source of potassium. Good brain and nerve food found in oil. Refer to Potassium Broth made from olives.
Onions, White Mineral	Sulphur Potassium		Peel onions under water to keep eyes from watering. Serve cooked or raw in salads.	Good for all catarrhal, bronchial, and lung disorders. *(Continued)*

55

Food and Type	Predominant Chemical Elements	Best Way Prepared and Served For Digestion	Remedial Measures
Oranges Mineral	Potassium Calcium Sodium Magnesium	To be used alone, with nuts, raw egg yolk, or with a protein meal. Juice or liquefy.	Good to stir up acids, catarrhal settlements and hard mucous.
Papaya Mineral	Sodium Magnesium Sulphur Chlorine	Eat as a melon or serve in salads. This makes juice divine.	Good for stomach and intestinal disorders, especially the seeds made into a tea.
Parsnips Mineral	Calcium Potassium Silicon	Wash, clean with stiff brush, cube, slice, or grate and steam. Makes a delicious taste when added to vegetable juice. Juice or liquefy.	Body mineralizer.
Parsley Mineral	Calcium Potassium Sulphur Iron	Eaten raw with salads, meats, soups, and vegetables. Used as tea, and in raw vegetable juice. Give your kidneys a break in juice form.	Good for diabetes, for cleansing the kidneys, for controlling calcium in the body. Body mineralizer.
Peaches Mineral	Calcium Phosphorus Potassium	Eaten alone, or in fruit salads with protein meal. Peach juice!!	Good bowel regulator. Body mineralizer and blood builder.
Peanuts Protein Fat Carbohydrate	Phosphorus Silicon Potassium	Eaten with green leafy salad. Raw peanuts are best.	Hard to digest.
Pears Mineral	Sodium Phosphorus	Eaten alone or in fruit salads with protein meals. Why not fresh pear juice?	Good body mineralizer. Good intestinal regulator. *(Continued)*

56

Food and Type	Predominant Chemical Elements	Best Way Prepared and Served For Digestion	Remedial Measures
Peas, Garbanzo Protein Carbohydrate	Magnesium Phosphorus	Eaten as protein. Cook as dried beans, such as lentils and navy beans. Soak before cooking.	Good source of vegetable protein.
Peas, Fresh Carbohydrate Mineral	Magnesium Calcium Chlorine	Shell and wash. Steam or use in broth. The pods also are good to use in broth with the peas. Liquefy.	Body mineralizer.
Pecans Protein Fat	Phosphorus Calcium Potassium	Best eaten with green vegetables or fruit, or flaked on breakfast fruits.	Good nut protein. Used in weight building with celery and apples.
Persimmons Mineral	Phosphorus Calcium	Eaten with other fresh fruit, protein, or alone. Use your imagination. Juice or liquefy.	Good body mineralizer. Good for irritable intestinal tract.
Pineapple Mineral	Sodium Calcium Magnesium Iodine	Eaten alone, with other fresh fruit, as in salad, or with protein. Good with so many juices. Juice or liquefy.	Good for sore throat, catarrhal conditions, good blood builder, aids digestion.
Plums Mineral	Magnesium	Eaten with other fresh fruit, alone, or with protein. Be careful—most are acid. Juice or liquefy.	Good laxative and bowel regulator.
Pomegranate Mineral	Sodium Magnesium	Squeeze out juice and drink very fresh. The best juice for urinary problems. Juice or liquefy.	Juice with whey is good in brain and nerve congestion. A blood cleanser. Juice for bladder complaints.
Popcorn Carbohydrate	Phosphorus	May be eaten with green leafy vegetable salad and a cream dressing.	Good for intestinal roughage.

(Continued)

57

Food and Type	Predominant Chemical Elements		Best Way Prepared and Served For Digestion	Remedial Measures
Potato, Baked Mineral Carbohydrate	Potassium Phosphorus Magnesium	Silicon	Clean with stiff brush. Parboil two minutes. Butter skins and bake in slow oven. Potato juice—peeling and all—marvelous!	Best source of starch. Use potato peeling in broths. Use for poultices.
Prunes Mineral	Potassium Phosphorus Magnesium		Wash, place in clean water, bring to boil, and let stand overnight. Use as dried fruit for breakfast, whipped for a dessert, or in salads. Get going—a be go-go person.	Good bowel regulator. Good source of nerve salts.
Pumpkin Carbohydrate	Sodium Iron Phosphorus		Eat with vegetable meal. Can be made into custards. Can be liquefied or juiced.	Body builder.
Radish, Black Mineral	Potassium Phosphorus Magnesium		Use as seasoning. Add a little sulfur or volcanic action to your juice.	Has Raphanon which is extremely good in gallbladder and liver disorders.
Radish, Red Mineral	Potassium Phosphorus Magnesium		Use raw in salads, with green vegetables and starches. Use both tops and bottoms in juicer.	Good source of sulphur. Good for catarrh.
Raisins Minerals	Potassium Phosphorus Chlorine		With vegetables, starch, or protein. Wash well. Soak. Use in cereals for sweetening or in salads.	Concentrated sweet. Good body builder and good energy food.
Raspberries Mineral	Sodium Iron		Wash well. Serve alone or with fruit or protein. Raspberry in other juices gets my O.K. Juice or liquefy.	Blood mineralizer. Neutralizes acidity. Good for anemia.
Rhubarb Mineral	Potassium Magnesium		Use steamed or baked with protein and raisins and apples to sweeten. Don't juice.	Spring cleanser of intestinal tract. *(Continued)*

58

Food and Type	Predominant Chemical Elements	Best Way Prepared and Served For Digestion	Remedial Measures
Rice, Natural Brown Carbohydrate	Phosphorus Sodium	Steam and serve with green vegetables.	Good body-building food. Good for bones, teeth, etc.
Rye, Whole Carbohydrate	Phosphorus Magnesium Silicon	Use with raw green vegetables.	Good source of silicon.
Spinach Mineral	Potassium Silicon	Cut off roots and dead leaves. Wash, cut fine, and use raw or steamed. Not too much because of high oxalic acid. Juice or liquefy.	Body mineralizer.
Squash Carbohydrate Mineral	Sodium Magnesium	Cut into pieces, or leave whole, and bake or steam. Let's have it.	Body builder, and bowel regulator.
Strawberries Mineral	Calcium Sodium	Wash, and use fresh with or without fruit or protein. Strawberries in a glass of juice. Juice or liquefy.	Acid neutralizer when eaten ripe.
Swiss Chard Mineral	Sodium Calcium Magnesium Iron	Wash thoroughly. Cut up in one-inch pieces. Steam. Tender sections may be used raw in salads. Juice it occasionally.	Body mineralizer.
Tomatoes Mineral	Potassium Sodium Chlorine	Use only ripest tomatoes. Use in salads, broths, or steamed. Use with proteins. Tomato juice with your proteins please. Liquefy.	Consider canned tomatoes best. Always use with a protein. Use also in packs and poultices.
Turnips Mineral Carbohydrate	Potassium Calcium	Wash and shred. Use raw in salads or serve steamed. Catarrhal problems respond to this juice. ⅓ juice in glass of other juices.	Body builder. White turnip juice good for asthma, sore throat and bronchial disorders. *(Continued)*

59

Food and Type	Predominant Chemical Elements	Best Way Prepared and Served For Digestion	Remedial Measures
Turnip Leaves Mineral	Calcium Magnesium	Serve raw in salads, in vegetable juices, or steam with greens. This juiced controls calcium in body.	Good for controlling calcium in body.
Walnut Protein Fat	Manganese Phosphorus Magnesium	To be used with fruit or vegetables in salads.	Black walnuts are best source of brain and nerve manganese food.
Watercress Mineral	Sulphur Chlorine Calcium	Wash well and use as salad green or garnish. Best for reducing. Juice or liquefy.	Body mineralizer.
Watermelon Mineral	Silicon Calcium Sodium	Use in fruit salads and protein meals, or serve alone. Best for kidneys. Juice or liquefy.	Good for kidneys. Blood cooler, and good source of silicon.
Wheat, Whole Carbohydrate	Phosphorus Silicon	Used in breads and cereals. Chew well, because starches must be mixed well with saliva in mouth to be digested properly.	Body builder of bone and teeth, especially for children. Best used in dry forms to promote vigorous chewing.
Whey Mineral	Sodium Calcium Chlorine	Add fruit juices to whey and drink two or three times daily between meals, drink alone, or with meals. Put your juice in whey for joint troubles.	Good source of mineral salts. Easy to digest, good blood builder. Important culture for the friendly bacteria in the intestinal tract.
Zucchini Mineral	Potassium	Wash, cut into pieces. Steam as vegetable or cut up raw in salads. A good food in a summer mixed juice.	Body mineralizer.

CHAPTER FIVE

VITAMINS AND MINERALS—
WHERE TO GET THEM

Sometimes I think we overestimate the importance of getting the right amounts of the right vitamins and minerals and underestimate the value of a balanced diet. If we ate the right foods, including plenty of whole grains, fruit, vegetables, raw seeds and raw nuts, we'd be getting enough vitamins and minerals without having to look up the amounts we're supposed to eat.

On the other hand, I've had a wonderful life finding out the facts of life about foods, and I want you to have fun using this book to get healthy with good juices and juice combinations.

So, here are the vitamins and minerals you need to know about to zero in on specific nutrients you might want to emphasize.

VITAMIN A

Pro-vitamin A, or beta carotene, is what we encounter in yellow fruits and green or yellow vegetables, and it is this substance that is transformed into the nature, fat-soluble vitamin A in the mucosa of the small intestine. Scientists tell us that pro-vitamin A is anticarcinogenic. Vitamin A is important to vision, growth, the reproductive system and the health of our mucous membranes. Deficiency is marked by night blindness, increased frequency of colds and catarrhal conditions, weight loss or failure to gain weight (in children) and loss of fertility.

The best fruit and vegetable sources of vitamin A are carrots, broccoli, tomatoes, asparagus, apricots, muskmelon, papayas, peaches, prunes, watermelon and all green, leafy vegetables.

VITAMIN B-COMPLEX

Symptoms of B-Complex deficiency may include fatigue, low energy, nervousness, depression, acne, insomnia, hair loss, skin disturbances and anemia, besides specific deficiency diseases such as beriberi and pellagra. (Excess alcohol and sugar consumption destroy B vitamins.)

Best sources of vitamin B-Complex are the green, leafy vegetables, wheat grass, barley grass, dandelion greens, sprouts, citrus, figs, berries and dates. Nearly all fruits and vegetables have *some* of the B-Complex vitamins but none that I know has vitamin B-12, so I recommend that the B-12 be obtained from chlorella tablets, available in health food stores. Chlorella is very high in vitamin B-12, and nearly all the recommended dietary allowance of this vitamin can be obtained by taking about 15 grams of chlorella. *(People who eat some meat, fish, poultry, eggs, cheese and various milk products every day, along with a generous supply of fruit, vegetables and whole cereal grains are likely to be getting all the B-Complex vitamins they need.)*

VITAMIN C

This vitamin is soluble in water and easily destroyed by exposure to air. Vitamin C is important in making collagen—the substance underlying skin, tendons, ligaments, cartilage and blood vessels. It works with iron to build the blood, helps make the neurotransmitter norepinephrine and has an antihistamine effect. Large amounts of vitamin C are found in the adrenal glands and are thought to have a lot to do with stress.

Vitamin C deficiency is signaled by poor digestion, bleeding gums, easy bruising, anemia, low resistance to infection, poor lactation in new mothers and shortness of breath. Chronic deficiency results in scurvy, which can be fatal if not treated. Standard treatment for scurvy is taking vitamin C-rich foods.

What foods are high in vitamin C? The highest I know are acerola berries, and after that, citrus fruits. Acerola, otherwise known as Barbados cherry, contains almost *four grams* of vitamin C in an 8-ounce cup of juice. In comparison, a cup of grapefruit juice has 93 milligrams of vitamin C and a cup of fresh orange juice has about 124 milligrams. Green, leafy vegetables have a modest amount of vitamin C, as do most tropical fruits, such as mangos, guavas and papayas. One guava, about 3-1/2 ounces in weight, has 240 milligrams of vitamin C. A cup of cauliflower has 78 milligrams, more than a large grapefruit. Asparagus, avocados, broccoli, Brussels sprouts, peas, red and green bell peppers, rutabagas and tomatoes have respectable amounts, as do apricots, bananas, blueberries, melons, strawberries and pineapple.

VITAMIN D

This vitamin, like vitamins A and E, is a fat-soluble vitamin. Nicknamed "the sunshine vitamin," vitamin D can be formed by the action of ultraviolet light from sunlight acting upon the cholesterol in the blood capillaries just under the skin. When supplementing your diet with this vitamin, stay out of the sun. With all the cholesterol in the average American diet, you would think most people would have plenty of vitamin D, but apparently that isn't the case. The precursors of vitamin D are found in both plants and animals, and we'll discuss the sources in a bit.

The reason vitamin D is so important is because it is necessary to bring in calcium through the intestinal wall, as well as phosphorus. Without these elements, the growth of bones and teeth in children is retarded. In adults, vitamin D helps maintain the nervous system, regulates blood-clotting capability and keeps the heartbeat stable. The largest supply of vitamin D in the body is found stored in the liver, but it is also found in the skin, spleen and brain.

Deficiency signs are soft bones, including rickets in children and osteomalacia in adults. Respiratory infections, restlessness and constipation may also be signs of deficiency. The RDA for vitamin D is 400 international units daily for those who spend most of their time indoors. Excess vitamin D can cause nausea, vomiting, diarrhea, weariness and calcification of soft tissues, which may lead to kidney failure.

Most nutrition researchers list only animal products as sources for vitamin D, such as fish, liver, butter and egg yolks. Fish liver oils are common sources for vitamins A and D. Most people are able to synthesize the vitamin D they need by getting a little sunlight every day. No fruit or vegetable sources of vitamin D are described or listed.

VITAMIN E

Vitamin E is not a single substance but a group of fat-soluble compounds called tocopherols, related chemically to alcohol. Heat will not break down vitamin E, but exposure to air will. Because vitamin E takes up oxygen slowly, it is able to protect fatty acids, other vitamins (like vitamins A and C) and enzymes from oxidation. This helps prevent the formation of free radicals like peroxides, which increase cancer risk and accelerate the symptoms of aging. The role of vitamin E in human sexuality is not well researched, but is assumed on the basis of animal experiments. Vitamin E is believed to assist in muscle function and is known to protect the liver from damage. Whether it helps relieve symptoms of heart disease isn't know, but it does play a part in blood coagulation.

Very little is known about deficiency symptoms of vitamin E because deficiency (at least identifiable deficiency) in normal people is unknown. Adults only need from 12 to 15 international units daily. One tablespoon of wheat germ oil has 21 milligrams of vitamin E. Eggs and leafy vegetables are considered good sources, as well as sprouts, leeks and cabbage.

VITAMIN K

Vitamin K is a blood-clotting factor found in alfalfa and other green vegetables, especially the leafy vegetables. It is probably abundant in wheat grass and barley grass as well.

When chemically isolated, vitamin K compounds are yellow oils that are not harmed by heat or air, but are destroyed by ultraviolet light. Cooking doesn't disturb it.

The only function vitamin K has is to help make the substance prothrombin in the liver.

Vitamin K is synthesized by beneficial bacteria in the intestinal tract and is found in a lot of food sources, including spinach, cabbage, kale and tomatoes. I don't know of any fruits that contain this vitamin.

FIBER

In the past two decades, Dr. Denis Burkitt, an English surgeon, has driven home the point that people with high-fiber diets have almost no colon cancer, diverticulosis, diabetes, ischemic heart disease or appendicitis. While fiber (both soluble and insoluble from fruits, vegetables, whole grains, nuts and seeds but *not from any animal sources*) is not an essential nutrient to preserve life, it is certainly needed in certain amounts to protect against malfunction, especially in the bowel.

Juice is wonderful, and juices (along with herbal teas) are among the fastest ways to take care of any vitamin or mineral deficiency in the body. But, the fiber in raw salads and raw blender drinks is, in my opinion, very, very important. I feel it is safe to say that very few people these days realize how much of our health, well-being and normal functioning of the body depends upon the bowel.

Constipation clogs the bowel, increases risk of diverticulosis and low-grade internal infection, and forces intestinal toxins that would normally be expelled from the body into the bloodstream.

To relieve the problem of constipation permanently requires dietary inclusion of more fiber foods every day. Eating supplementary fiber is not the best solution. Making more fiber foods a regular part of our food regimen is the best solution.

Chapter 8 is titled Blending Naturally for Health and Wellness, and I urge you, for health's sake, to make high-fiber foods part of your daily diet.

Here are some wonderful high-fiber foods to include in your daily food plan, and the amount of fiber they have.

Food	**% Fiber**	**Food**	**% Fiber**
Bananas	22.0	Carrot	8.9
Pears	15.3	Tomatoes	6.6
Oranges	9.9	Green beans	12.4
Apples	14.9	Potato	4.0

The water-holding ability of cellulose fiber not only softens the stool and allows better peristaltic movement, but the fiber tends to carry out more heavy metals and cholesterol as bowel transit time is reduced.

 **CALCIUM**

Calcium gives vitality, endurance, heals wounds, counteracts acid, is tone-building in the body and, of course, builds and

maintains bone structure and teeth, where needed most. Calcium is the knitting element, and blood-clotting problems indicate a calcium deficiency. The metabolism of calcium needs vitamin F (essential fatty acids). Principal sources are bran and cheese (very high), raw goat's milk, Swiss, Dutch edam or gouda cheese, milk, raw egg yolk, figs, prunes, dates, onion, kale, cauliflower, bone meal, turnip greens, kidney beans, soybeans and lentils.

(C) CARBON

Carbon is the principal element for growth. Wherever carbon and oxygen are at work, one upon the other, there is heat generation, growth and generation of carbonic acid gas. Carbon is the basic element of cell birth and cell life, and mainly supports the vital systems. An excess results in obesity, boils, fatty degeneration, anemia, high blood pressure. Carbon or its compounds, as a food, occur mainly in starch, sweets, fats and also in most proteins. To counteract an excess, avoid fatty foods such as fatty game meats, oily fish, goose, fatty sausage and gravies. Foods low in fat are bass, bone broth, buttermilk, skimmed milk, goat's milk cheese and cottage cheese, cauliflower, young carrots, tender cabbage, chard, string beans, blueberries and blackberries.

(Cl) CHLORINE

Found and needed mostly in the digestive system and secretions. It is the cleanser in the body, expels waste, freshens, purifies, disinfects. Deficiency contributes to sluggish liver and glandular swellings. Goat's milk provides chlorine effective in kidney problems because of its germicidal effect. Other principal sources are raw milk, fish, cheese, coconut, beets, radishes, dry figs, endive, watercress, cucumber, carrots, leeks,

Roquefort cheese, Danish blue cheese, Swiss cheese and Italian cheese and all green vegetables.

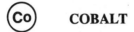 **COBALT**

Cobalt is the essential trace element needed to form vitamin B-12 by bacterial action in the small intestine. It also activates certain enzymes in the body. If the bacteria in the bowel are unable to produce B-12, it may be because of an unfavorable surplus of undesirable bacterial stimulated by use of chronic imbalanced diet or use of antibiotics. In such a case, even the availability of cobalt doesn't necessarily mean that B-12 can be formed, which means that a vitamin B-12 supplement will have to be taken to prevent anemia from developing.

Green, leafy vegetables and ripe fruits are acceptable sources of cobalt. You might want to call your county agricultural commissioner's office and find out if the soil in your area contains cobalt. If it doesn't, try to get out-of-the-area produce.

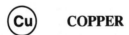 **COPPER**

Copper, like cobalt, is an essential trace element involved in the formation and upkeep of the red blood cell population. It is needed for certain enzymes and may play a role in maintaining the integrity of the myelin sheath surrounding the nerves. Recent research shows that copper deficiency may stimulate the breakdown of joint membranes and contribute to the inflammation associated with arthritis.

Copper deficiency may be indicated in anemia as well as in the onset of joint problems, as previously mentioned.

Not much copper is needed, and it is supplied by raw beets, beet greens, greens in general, onions, parsley, carrots, broccoli, celery, green peppers, pineapple, prunes, quince, berries and melons.

(FI) FLUORINE

Found and needed mostly in the structural system, tooth enamel and to preserve bones. It is a disease resister and beautifier in the body, strengthens tendons and knits bones. Fluorine combines with calcium. It is stored in the spleen, eye structure and elastic tissues. Fluorine is destroyed by high temperatures. Raw goat's milk contains highest content of fluorine. Other principal sources are cauliflower, cabbage, cheese, cow's milk, raw egg yolk, cod liver oil, Brussels sprouts, spinach, tomatoes, watercress, salad vegetables and black bass.

(H) HYDROGEN

Present in bodily secretions, soft tissue, lymph, brain, lungs, glands, liver, kidneys, spleen, pancreas. Hydrogen foods are the moisture-carrying foods such as apricots, cherries, all berries, fruit juices, cabbage, tomatoes, leaf lettuce, Swiss chard, watercress and so forth. The nerves must be bathed in fresh moisture. Without hydrogen, the blood could not flow and waste toxic materials could not be washed out of the body; however, an excess of water in the body causes pressure and enlargement of bodily organs.

(I) IODINE

A gland and brain element. It is a metabolism normalizer in the body: prevents goiter; normalizes gland and cell action; ejects and counteracts poisons. Indications of iodine deficiency are claustrophobia, fears, flabby arms, pronunciation difficulties and mental depression. Iodine is very high in sea lettuce, sea kelp foods, carrots, pears, onions, tomatoes, pineapple, potato skin, cod liver oil, garlic, watercress, green leek soup, clam juice and nettle tea.

(Fe) IRON

Essential in the blood as the oxygen carrier; prevents anemia; promotes vitality and ambition. Iron foods attract oxygen. Indications of iron deficiencies are weakness, lassitude, skin eruptions, leukorrhea, tendency for crying, personal magnetism often fails, asthma problems, bronchitis and hemorrhages. Principal sources are all green, leafy vegetables, wild blackberries and black cherries, egg yolk, liver, oysters, potato peeling broth, whole wheat, parsley, parsnips, spinach, Swiss chard, goat's brown cheese, artichokes, asparagus, nettle tea, leeks, lamb's lettuce, white onions, rice bran, whole rye meal and salad greens.

(Mg) MAGNESIUM

Nature's laxative, a nerve mineral, found and needed mostly in the digestive system. It prevents and relieves autointoxication; refreshes the system; and is a new-cell promoter in the body. Indications of magnesium deficiency are temper, over excitement and excessive emotion. Principal sources are grapefruit, oranges, figs, whole barley, corn, yellow cornmeal, wheat bran, coconut, goat's milk and raw egg yolk.

Fruits containing significant amounts of magnesium include apples, apricots, bananas, avocados, passion fruit, loganberries, mangos, nectarines, peaches and pears. Dried fruits are very high in magnesium. All green vegetables are high in magnesium, because magnesium is at the center of every chlorophyll molecule, and chlorophyll is what makes plants green.

(Mn) MANGANESE

A memory element, tissue strengthener for linings of body structure, increases resistance, improves memory, coordinates thought and action and needed mostly in the nervous system. Manganese is dependent on iron and phosphorus. It is involved in normal skeletal development.

Deficiency symptoms include convulsions, dizziness, facial neuralgia, angry and silent moods, rectal cramps after meals, blindness, paralysis, poor muscle coordination and even loss of hearing.

Principle sources of manganese are nasturtium leaves, raw egg yolk, almonds, black walnuts, watercress, mint, parsley, wintergreen, endive. Vegetable sources of manganese include kale, kohlrabi, parsley, onions, beets, eggplant, leafy greens (especially spinach), tomatoes and broccoli. Fruits include pineapple, raspberries, apples, avocados, bananas and red currants.

(N) NITROGEN

As found in food or in air, it is a restraining element, the opposite of oxygen. Oxygen is like fire. Nitrogen is stillness itself. Without nitrogen, oxygen would burn us up and we would cease to exist. Nitrogen enters human tissue under many different names in the solid elastic tissue, lymph, muscles, blood plasma, the crystalline lenses of the eyes, connective tissues, mucous membranes, skin, hair, nails and so forth. The main supply of nitrogen is found in proteins, the principal muscle builder. Nitrogen yields heat and muscular energy. A deficiency leads to muscular exhaustion, numbness, tired feelings; however, an excess of nitrogen results in autointoxication, stagnation, swelling, forgetfulness, headache, enlargement of heart, etc. It is very important to keep nitrogen in proper balance. Nitrogen or very high protein foods are almonds, beans, beef, fish, goat's cheese, lean veal, liver, quail, cheese, unleavened breads. Low-nitrogen foods are young kale, milk whey, okra, ripe olives, parsley, apricots, artichokes, string beans, young carrots, romaine lettuce, tomatoes, turnips, wild cherry juice, wintergreen, etc.

(O) OXYGEN

Oxygen infiltrates each individual cell in the body, influencing building and demolishing processes; it affects each individual differently according to the other chemical elements in the body.

An ample supply of oxygen is needed in order to supply the lungs, blood and tissues, keep the arteries elastic, eyes glowing, heart active and agile. Some of the high-oxygen foods are: liquid chlorophyll, iron tonics, red juicy meats, beets, grapes, tomatoes, onions, leeks, wild cherry juice, etc. The best oxygen "foods" for the respiratory system are fresh mountain air, clean air and higher altitudes.

(P) PHOSPHORUS

Found and needed mostly in the nervous system and is a brain and bone element. This is a nerve builder and nourishes the brain, builds power of thought, stimulates growth of hair and bone, helps thinking processes and intelligence. Indications of phosphorus deficiency are loss of patience, neurosis, craving excitement, psychosis, fears and anxiety. Phosphorus and sulfur foods should be eaten together and are controlled by iodine. Phosphorus also needs more oxygen. An excess will cause weak kidneys and lungs. Principal sources of phosphorus are seafoods, milk, raw egg yolk, parsnips, whole wheat, barley, yellow corn, nuts, peas, beans and lentils.

(K) POTASSIUM

A tissue and secretion chemical element, found and needed mostly in the digestive system. Potassium is a healer in the body; a liver activator; makes tissues elastic and muscles supple; creates grace, beauty and a good disposition. Potassium is strongly alkaline. Indications of deficiency are a desire for cold foods, sour foods and acid drinks. Principal sources are potato skins, dandelion, dill, sage, dried olives, parsley, blueberries, peaches, prunes, coconut, gooseberries, cabbage, figs and almonds.

(Se) SELENIUM

Selenium is a trace element that works with vitamin E in the body to prevent the formation of free radicals, which, in turn, protects cell nuclear DNA from being damaged and lowers the risk of cancer. Selenium helps keep tissues elastic by helping protect fatty acids from oxidation. The greatest concentrations of selenium are found in the liver and kidneys.

Selenium deficiency may be indicated by symptoms of premature aging.

Vegetables containing selenium include tomatoes, onions, green beans, cabbage, carrots, cauliflower, garlic, lotus root, green bell peppers and possibly other vegetables grown in soil containing selenium. Without selenium in the soil, there is no selenium in the plant. Among the fruits, citrus, peaches, pears, apples, bananas, dates and red currants contain selenium, if grown where selenium is in the soil.

(Si) SILICON

Found and needed mostly in the structural system, nails, skin, teeth, hair and the ligaments. Silicon creates a magnetic quality and is the "surgeon" in the body, giving keen hearing, sparkling eyes, hard teeth, glossy hair, tones the system and gives resistance to the body. Silicon is especially important for the agility in the body for walking and dancing. Indications of silicon deficiency are coordination problems, fungus diseases, parched lips, feeling of approaching death, impotence and sexual disability. Principal sources of silicon are oats, barley, brown rice, rye, corn, peas, beans, lentils, wheat, spinach, asparagus, lettuce, tomatoes, cabbage, figs, strawberries, oat straw tea, watermelon seeds and peelings, coconut, sage, thyme, hops, prunes, bone marrow, raw egg yolk, pecans, cod liver oil, halibut liver oil.

(Na) SODIUM

A gland, ligament and blood builder found and needed mostly in the digestive system. Sodium is the youth maintainer in the body; aids digestion; counteracts acidosis; halts fermentation; purifies blood; forms saliva, bile and the pancreatic juices. Flexibility of tendons needs high-sodium foods, and sodium aids the intestinal flora. Indications of deficiency are restlessness, depression, nervousness, poor concentration, tender abdominal muscles, sore cervical glands, puffiness in face and body, and an inactive spleen. Principal sources are okra, celery, carrots, beets, cucumbers, asparagus, turnips, strawberries, oat meal, raw egg yolk, coconut, black figs, spinach, sprouts, peas, goat's cheese and milk, goat's whey, fish, oysters, clams, lobster, milk and lentils.

(S) SULFUR

A brain and tissue chemical element, found and needed mostly in the nervous system. Sulfur tones the system, purifies and activates the body, intensifies feelings and emotions. Sulfur needs iodine to work properly. Driving force for goals and achievements is stimulated by sulfur foods. Indications of sulfur deficiency are fretting, pouting, retiring late and rising early, poor appetite in the morning, extremes of variety and change, anemic-looking skin. Indication of excess sulfur is face burning, and an excess indicates need for chlorine and magnesium foods. Principal sources of sulfur are cabbage, cauliflower, onions, asparagus, carrots, horseradish, shrimp, chestnuts, mustard greens, radishes, spinach, leeks, garlic, apples, turnips and beet tops, plums, prunes, apricots, peaches, raw egg yolk and melons.

(Zn) ZINC

Zinc is a trace element involved in many enzyme reactions in the digestion and metabolism of nutrients. It is a necessary part of insulin, which is crucial in controlling blood sugar levels and the storage of excess sugar.

Nucleic acid formation requires zinc, as does the proper working of the male prostate gland. It is required for growth and healing.

Zinc deficiency may be characterized by slow growth, a delay in sexual maturity, slow healing, sterility, fatigue, poor alertness and being prone to infection.

Asparagus is high in zinc, and beets have a little. Spinach, green peppers and Brussels sprouts are good as vegetables go, but nuts and seeds are the real powerhouses—especially Brazil nuts, cashews, hazelnuts and both English and black walnuts. Consider adding one or more of these raw nuts to a vegetable juice (containing zinc) and combining the two to increase the total zinc. Raw pumpkin seeds are the highest source of zinc I know. Fruit sources include apples, avocados, cantaloupe, citrus, mangos and peaches.

SOME OBSERVATIONS ON JUICES

In most cases, juicing a fruit or vegetable will concentrate the vitamins and minerals in the juice, especially in the case of water-soluble nutrients.

Apple juice serves as a convenient base to mix either other fruit or vegetable juices.

Seed and nut milks are compatible with either fruit or vegetable juices to enrich the mineral content.

Children are more likely to drink juice than they are to eat the fruit or vegetables.

JUICE COMPARISON CHART

ITEM	Amt. (cup)	Wt. % (gram)	Cal.	A	B₁	B₂	B₃	B₆	B₁₀ (mcg)	B₁₂ (mcg)	Folic	Panto. Acid
Tomato Juice	1	242	46	1,940	0.12	0.07	1.9	0.37	.0	0	0.02	0.61
Vegetable Juice Cocktail	1	242	41	1,690	0.12	0.07	1.9	—	—	—	—	—
Sauerkraut Juice	1	242	24	—	0.07	0.10	0.5	0.61	—	0	—	0.29
Carrot Juice	1	227	96	24,750	0.13	0.12	0.6	0.5	2.0	0	0.002	0.20
Acerola Juice (Barbados Cherry)	1	242	56	—	0.05	0.15	1.0	0.01	—	0	—	0.49
Apple Juice	1	248	117	—	0.02	0.05	0.2	0.08	1.2	0	0.002	0.05
Apricot Nectar	1	251	143	2,380	0.03	0.03	0.5	—	—	0	—	—
Blackberry Juice	1	245	91	—	0.05	0.07	0.7	—	—	0	—	0.2
Grapefruit Juice	1	250	98	200	0.1	0.05	0.5	0.03	1.7	0	0.05	0.3
Lemon Juice	1	250	66	—	—	—	—	0.01	—	—	—	0.25
Lime Juice	1	250	65	—	—	—	—	—	—	0	—	0.76
Orange Juice, fresh	1	248	112	500	0.22	0.07	1.0	1.0	0.8	0	0.14	0.47
Orange Juice, frozen	1	249	122	540	0.23	0.03	0.9	0.07	—	0	0.14	0.41
Papaya Juice, canned	1	250	120	5,000	0.04	0.02	0.2	—	—	—	0.01	—
Pineapple Juice	1	250	138	130	0.13	0.05	0.5	—	—	—	0.003	0.25
Prune Juice	1	256	197	—	0.03	0.03	1.0	—	—	—	—	—

(continued on next page)

JUICE COMPARISON CHART (continued)

ITEM	AMT. (cup)	WT. % (gram)	CAL.	C	E	Na	K	Phos.	Ca.	Fe.	Mg.	Zn.
Tomato Juice	1	242	46	39	–	486	552	44	17	2.2	20.0	0.1
Vegetable Juice Cocktail	1	242	41	22	–	484	535	53	29	1.2	–	–
Sauerkraut Juice	1	242	24	44	–	1,905	–	34	30	2.7	–	–
Carrot Juice	1	227	96	3	–	366	186	34	47	1.1	7.0	0.5
Acerola Juice (Barbados Cherry)	1	242	56	3,872	–	7	–	22	24	1.2	–	–
Apple Juice	1	248	117	2	–	2	250	22	15	1.5	10.0	–
Apricot Nectar	1	251	143	8	–	1	379	30	23	0.5	–	–
Blackberry Juice	1	245	91	25	–	2	417	29	29	2.2	51.5	–
Grapefruit Juice	1	250	98	95	0.1	2	405	36	22	0.5	30.0	0.08
Lemon Juice	1	250	66	115	–	–	344	39	16	–	2.0	0.03
Lime Juice	1	250	65	81	–	–	259	32	16	–	13.0	–
Orange Juice, fresh	1	248	112	124	–	2	496	42	27	0.5	49.0	0.09
Orange Juice, frozen	1	249	122	120	–	2	503	42	25	0.2	25.0	0.09
Papaya Juice, canned	1	250	120	111	–	–	–	24	44	0.8	–	–
Pineapple Juice	1	250	138	23	–	3	373	23	38	0.8	30.0	–
Prune Juice	1	256	197	5	–	5	602	51	36	10.5	26.0	0.03

CHAPTER SIX

JUICING FOR LIFE

You need to realize that juicing is not just one of those things you should pick up and lay down when you want to. Not only the quality of your life depends on regularly meeting your body's nutrient needs, but its longevity. And, longevity is relatively meaningless when life degenerates into one disease, disturbance and doctor bill after another. Longevity and a high quality of life together are precious.

One of the reasons I'm so glad to see a juice trend catching on in this country is that it may signal a move away from overeating protein, fatty foods, salty foods and dairy products that I believe are killing us. I still hear too many men saying, "I'm a meat-and-potatoes man," although not as much as I used to hear it.

Another reason I'm favorably impressed with people who are joining the juicing movement is that I believe a genuine concern for better health is taking place, in the very face of health care costs so high that none but the rich (or the well insured) can financially survive a lengthy hospital stay. One way to lower health care costs is for more people to stay healthy and keep out of hospitals and doctors' offices.

OTHER LANDS, OTHER PEOPLE

In all my travels, the places where I've found the oldest living persons—like the Hunza Valley, the Caucasus mountains, Turkey, Villacabamba and others—were never urban, never highly cultured, never populated by the rich and famous.

People born in high-poverty areas with rich soil and limited amounts of food don't eat sparingly and simply because they want to, they do it because they have to. This is one of their secrets—they have to eat sparingly and they have to work very hard every day. Do we have to be compelled to do what's good and what's right for ourselves? It's something I'm concerned about, because conditions seem to be degenerating worldwide.

One of the old men I talked to in the Caucasus mountains of the former U.S.S.R. answered my questions through an interpreter. I asked, "What did you do to reach such a wonderful age?" "Nothing," he said. "I didn't know I was going to live this long." I think he was 147 years old at the time I talked to him.

GOOD HEALTH MUST BE EARNED

I realize that juices and juicing are a wonderful trend, but I hope you and your friends realize that good health is not a gift from the Creator, but an opportunity to express your appreciation for the gift of life by working hard every day to sustain high-level well-being.

The true joy of life is only real joy if it can be expressed in a state of health in which the quality of life is understood and appreciated. It's hard to feel wonderful when you feel terrible, if you know what I mean. And the right way to take care of our aches and pains is to prevent them from taking hold in our lives by choosing to live the right way, by choosing to take the higher path.

Good health must be earned. Do you know of anything else more worth working for than your own good health?

I hope you continue to enjoy juicing, but I hope you will also stop and take a minute to think about your health and your life.

Do you want to stay healthy as you grow older? Do you want to have the energy and motivation to live an interesting life and meet your goals with a sense of meaningful achievement?

Remember, you are juicing for life, and if you want that life to stay as nice as it is, make a commitment to enter into the kind of lifestyle that has satisfaction and happiness as two of its main side effects.

CHAPTER SEVEN

CHILDREN AND JUICES

We find that the nutrition intake of the pregnant mother-to-be is what determines the nutrition intake of the developing embryo, and the juices described in this book, taken by the mother, can assist in providing the varfiety of vitamins, enzymes, minerals and other nutrients to assure the best of health to both mother and child during and after labor and delivery. I personally feel it is better to get vitamins and minerals from foods than from pills.

After the baby is delivered, mother's milk is the best food for the newborn. For the first three days of breast feeding, a protein--rich fluid called colostrum is taken by the baby, which provides the globulins and other immune factors to protect the child from a broad variety of diseases and afflictions, until its own immune system is fully functional.

During the first few months of its life, the baby's nutritional intake is obtained from the milk it drinks, and if it can't have mother's milk, it should have fresh, raw goat's milk, which is the closest to mother's milk. As long as the baby is being breast fed, however, the mother should drink 2 cups of carrot, celery and parsley juices, mixed, daily. If she needs more milk production for the baby, she should have more greens in juice form or in the regular diet. This will help make sure that the mother's milk includes all the nutrients the baby needs.

WHEN SHOULD INFANTS BEGIN TAKING JUICES?

Mother's milk is a whole food, able to provide all nutrients needed by the newborn, but the time comes when there is not enough of it to match the growth needs of the child. This is the time when the baby will need to take a little solid food. (I recommend that you make these at home from organically-grown cereal grains, fruit, vegetables, etc. There are books available to tell you how to make fresh baby food, **with no chemical additives**.) There also comes a time when juices are a timely and wise addition to an infant's early nutritional intake.

The best way, I think, to estimate when your baby is ready for his or her first juices is when the birth weight has doubled (or more) to at least 14 pounds, and the baby is breast feeding 8-to-12 times per day or taking at least 32 ounces of milk by bottle. Some doctors use other criteria—such as the age of 6 months, or whenever the infant is able to handle drinking from a cup with a lid and spout.

The first juices you should give your baby are apple, white grape and pear. Juice these yourself for highest nutritional value, and make sure the pulp is strained out. Dilute half-and-half with distilled water, or reverse oxmosis water.

I also recommend, at this juncture in your baby's life, that you add a teaspoon of green vegetable juice to the baby's bottle of milk once every two days. The juice may be from raw spinach, broccoli, parsley or wheat grass. **Use only one teaspoon because the green juice is very concentrated and potent.** The green juice will provide iron (which is deficient in milk), electrolytes and chlorophyll, which will feed the beneficial bowel flora. Iron deficiency anemia is not uncommon in infants over 6 months who are given lots of milk and few solids.

Juice combinations such as apple-guava, carrot-celery, apple-carrot, carrot-milk, mango-apple, pear-prune and others can be given when your baby reaches 18 pounds. I do not encourage the use of citrus juices because they are too alkaline-forming in the stomach.

If your baby reacts to a particular juice by vomiting or diarrhea, wait another month or so and try again. If the vomiting or diarrhea reappears, talk to your doctor about it.

As the baby gets older and grows larger, gradually use less water in the juices until you are using all juice. Your baby will usually triple in weight the first year, and its height will increase by 50%.

When your baby has indigestion or stomach gas (burping more than usual), try a little diluted papaya juice.

For diarrhea, blackberry or blueberry juice may bring relief. Dilute for babies, but use undiluted juice for infants over a year old.

I don't want to give the impression that your goal should be to work toward giving your child undiluted pure juice as soon as possible. Not at all! Some juices will always be so strong that they should be taken diluted with some milder juice, or with raw goat's milk. Green juice, whether from broccoli, spinach, kale or wheat grass, should always be diluted three-to-one with a milder juice such as carrot, carrot-celery, apple or apple-carrot. The wonderful advantage of mixing juices is that you can almost always find a combination that is pleasing (or at least acceptable) to your child.

OLDER CHILDREN CAN HELP

The way to get older boys and girls interested in juicing and juices is to invite them to help. Juicing, supervised and assisted by an adult, is an exciting challenge to children. The adult should be the one to cut fruit into juicer-acceptable chunks, unless the child is old enough, skilled enough and responsible enough to be allowed to use a knife. When kids help, they usually want to sample the different juice combinations to find out how they taste. If you offered them some of the same juices in a glass, without their participation, many kids would say no—especially to vegetable juices. But, usually, you can find a way to make even the most bland, bitter or sharp-tasting vegetable juice acceptable to your child by diluting it with enough apple juice to make the flavor more fruit-like. Children like fruit flavors more than they do vegetable flavors.

Apple juice or carrot juice can be mixed with almost any other fruit or vegetable juice to make it taste better.

Don't try to cram a lot of nutrition information into your five-year old or even your fourteen-year old, for that matter. Let them ask the questions, and they'll get farther into it themselves without you doing any persuading or insisting.

One of the greatest ways of pouring in all the vitamins, minerals, enzymes and other nutrients your child needs to stay healthy and full of life is to get him or her into the habit of drinking foiur glasses of different juices every day.

Among the most important groups of chemical elements needed by every growing child are the electrolytes, which include sodium, potassium, calcium, magnesium, chloride, phosphate and bicarbonate. Juices, like human body fluids, are charged with electrically-active chemical elements and molecules. The electrolytes play a very important part in making the human body healthy and active, and we can get these vital nutrients from juices.

ROLE OF JUICES IN PROVIDING WATER AND ELECTROLYTES

A sufficient supply of electrolytes is very important in your child's health, and you can keep their electrolytes up with juices. Most body fluids contain a rich population of chemicals called electrolytes, which are electrically-charged chemical elements. These electrified particles assist in the passage of nutrients into cells and wastes out of cells, through the cell membranes. They help in the transport of nutrients through the bowel wall and in transmission of nerve signals. Electrolytes take part in thousands of chemical processes in the body that take place by electrical interactions. The most common cause of electrolyte deficiency in children is prolonged vomiting or diarrhea for several days. Consult your doctor in all cases of persisting vomiting or diarrhea.

Water. A newborn baby is nearly 75% water, which is the basic liquid substance of the blood, lymph, tears, saliva, urine, spinal fluid and almost all other body fluids. Chemical reactions, body temperature and lubrication of all membranes depends on water. Deficiency symptoms include thirst and fever. Excess signs include headache, nausea, cramps, convulsion, vomiting and diluted, watery urine. **All juices are good sources of water.**

Calcium. Infants need calcium for the development of bones and teeth, for proper muscle contraction, nerve stability, regular heartbeat and for blood clotting. Calcium shortage is signaled by numbness or tingling of the fingertips, toes, nose and ears. Calcium excess is hard to detect. While both babies and infants usually get enough milk to supply plenty of calcium, it may not be in proper balance with vitamins A, C and D and the iron, magnesium, manganese and phosphorus needed to make calcium use in the body most effective. Two parts calcium to one part magnesium and 2.5 parts calcium to one part phosphorus are the best ratios. **Best juices for proper calcium use in the body are mixed juices—three parts carrot juice with one part kale, spinach or broccoli juice and a teaspoon of wheat grass juice. All green vegetables are high in calcium, magnesium, manganese, iron, phosphorus,** as well as vitamins A and C. Vitamin D is usually made in the infant's body as it is exposed to direct or indirect sunlight for a few minutes each day.

Sodium. The level of sodium in the body determines the amount of water that will be retained, the acid-base balance and the cellular osmosis. Sodium works with potassium in regulating osmosis, and works with the electrolyte bicarbonate in regulating the acid-alkaline balance. Nerve transmission also requires sodium and potassium working together. Too little sodium in the body would result in nausea, vomiting, headaches, weakness and cramps. Too much sodium causes water retention with tissue bloating, irregular heartbeat and overexcitement. **Sodium is highest in okra, celery, tomatoes and sun-ripened fruits.**

Potassium. Twice as much potassium as sodium is needed by the body. Potassium works with sodium to maintain acid-alkaline balance, osmotic balance and regulation of water. Potassium is needed by all muscles and for starch and protein metabolism. Deficiency is shown by anxiety, apathy, lack of energy, muscle weakness, nausea and irregular heartbeat. Too much would cause colic, diarrhea and nausea. **Potassium is most abundant in green vegetables and fruit.**

Chlorine. Osmotic pressure is affected by chlorine, which works with sodium and potassium. Chlorine deficiency occurs only after an extended siege of vomiting or diarrhea. Excess is seldom found. **Adequate supply of chlorine is found in almost all juices.**

Magnesium. The hardening of bones, neutralizing of muscle acids and participation in energy production processes makes magnesium an essential element for children of all ages. Deficiency is rare, but prolonged diarrhea can cause it, and so can kidney disease. Symptoms are muscle twitching, tremors, facial muscle spasms, convulsions, apathy and confusion. Excess of magnesium is extremely rare and seldom observed. **All green vegetables are excellent sources of magnesium.**

Phosphate. Phosphorus combines with oxygen to form electrically-charged phosphate molecules. Phosphates are essential to building healthy bones and teeth, transport of fats in the blood, the metabolism of fats, sugars and starches, and energy production. Deficiency cause rickets, excess causes loss of calcium and muscle spasms. **Phosphorus is found in all fruits and vegetables.**

Bicarbonate. This electrolyte is a carbonic acid salt containing hydrogen, carbon and oxygen, and it is important in maintaining every child's acid-alkaline balance. Deficiency may be indicated by excessive water or electrolyte loss, while too much bicarbonate causes high-blood sugar and liver disturbances. Bicarbonates are synthesized in the process of respiration and we are not dependent on foods to supply them.

JUICES ARE FOODS

We have to keep in mind that juices are foods, despite the fact that we use them as a supplementary backup, to fill in the missing nutrients we may not have gotten in our regular diet. Remember, some people can't digest, or can't assimilate all the solid foods that would usually provide for their needs. That's where juices pick up the slack, so to speak.

Nutrients from juices are digested easily and assimilated quickly, flooding all the constitutionally weak organs, glands and tissues with the vital nutrients needed to prevent deficiencies and support a healthy lifestyle.

You owe it to your children's health and future well-being to teach them about juices and juicing and to get them started now.

SECTION II

BLENDING NATURALLY
FOR HEALTH AND WELLNESS

CHAPTER EIGHT

BLENDING NATURALLY
FOR HEALTH AND WELLNESS

Unlike juicers, which separate the liquid of the fruit or vegetable from the pulp, blenders liquefy the food completely. Blenders are especially good for creating combinations—juices with solids, different fruits or vegetables, fruits with seeds or nuts and so forth. Liquefied foods and combinations are not digested and assimilated as fast as juices, but they are taken up faster than a meal of solid foods. And, they provide fiber for the bowel.

The main advantage of liquefied foods is that you can combine foods that have the specific nutrient combinations you want, which may not be available in a single vegetable or fruit.

Selecting and buying a blender that will meet your needs takes the same kind of thought and research as buying a juicer. I suggest that you go to the library and read the consumer magazines or books on blenders, to get an idea of relative prices and performances, then go to several health food stores and talk to the clerk about the kind of blender that would be best for you.

The following ideas are from my book *Blending Magic*, which has many more recipes than these and can be ordered by mail.

BLENDER DRINK BASES

For fruit drinks, choose your liquid base from the fruit juices, as they add flavor and value: Apple, grape, pineapple (unsweetened), blackberry, elderberry, pomegranate, mulberry, wild cherry, blueberry, raspberry.

For vegetable drinks, try to choose a vegetable base: Carrot, celery, mixed greens, etc. Tomato juice, liquid chlorophyll (usually from alfalfa) available at your local health food store. One teaspoon to one cup water. Whey (powdered) 1 tbsp to 1 cup water.

Herb teas with leaves or seeds, such as fenugreek or alfalfa. Select according to preference or for any particular medicinal need, as papaya for beneficial effect on kidneys and digestion of proteins; comfrey for general healing and for bowels; huckleberry for starch digestion or camomile. Oat straw tea is mild.

Vegetable broth seasoning, 1 tsp to about 1 cup water. Makes an excellent protein drink base.

For both fruit and vegetable drinks, you can use goat's milk as a base, as well as raw cow's milk, soy milk, coconut and nut milks.

Drinking raw vegetable cocktails is one of the best ways of supplying needed minerals to the body. They should not be used in place of raw vegetable salads, but rather to supplement them. Drink them at any time of the day or with any meal. Any water left over after steaming vegetables should be used in cocktail bases, never discarded.

SWEETENERS

Soaked raisins, dates, figs or sweet prunes are wonderful for improving taste; soaked black walnuts are also very good to cover a "nasty" taste. The presence of solid particles makes vegetable juices conducive to chewing. These are concentrated foods and not to be taken as a "drink." *They should be chewed to mix with the saliva.*

Unsulfured molasses has healthful properties for use as sweetener in beverages. Also use date sugar, maple syrup or carob powder.

PROTEIN DRINKS

Make protein drinks by adding cottage cheese, egg yolk, nut butters and milks, pre-ground nuts and seeds, soy powder, protein or amino-acid powders and other prepared supplements.

CARBOHYDRATE DRINKS

Add barley or other whole grains, cooked or soaked. Baked potato with the skin is a good way to use up leftovers—with one or two root vegetables, leeks, green, leafy vegetables, parsley, herbs and seasoning.

For an especially nutritious drink, have one of the nut or seed milks, carrot milk or banana milk.

VEGETABLE DRINKS

Vegetable Cocktail

Blend until liquefied, to serve 3-4:

2 C tomato juice
1 sml stalk celery
  w/leaves, cut up
2-3 sprigs of
  parsley
2 slices lemon

1 slice green pepper
1 slice onion
1/4 tsp vegetable broth
  seasoning
1/2 tsp honey
1 C cracked ice

Beet Borscht Drink

1/3 C carrot juice   1/4 C cucumber juice
1/3 C beet juice   1 tbsp lemon juice
Blend and serve with spoonful of sour cream or yogurt on top.

Carrot Juice Cocktail

Liquefy:
1 C carrot juice   2 sprigs parsley
1/4 C any green juice   1/2 tsp vegetable broth
 and/or 1-2 green leaves   seasoning or any de-
 (outer leaves of endive   sired herb for flavoring
 or romaine are good)

Garden-Fresh Tomato Juice

Bring really ripe tomatoes in off your vines, rinse, slice and
blend without adding liquid. A little vegetable broth seasoning
may be added, and a pinch of your favorite herb. Once well
blended, strain through a fine sieve; chill.

Watercress Cocktail

Blend until watercress is liquefied.
2 C pineapple juice   1 thick slice lemon or
 unsweetened   2 tbsp lemon juice
1 bunch watercress   1 C cracked ice
3 tbsp honey or raw sugar

Borscht-Yogurt Drink

Blend velvety smooth in liquefier. If desired, pulp may be
strained through sieve. Top with spoonful of sour cream.
1 C yogurt   1/2 C diced carrot
1/2 sml lemon, peeled,   1/4 diced cucumber
 seeded   1 tsp vegetable broth
1/2 C diced beets   seasoning

Carrot-Parsley Cocktail

Liquefy to serve one:
2/3 C carrot juice   6 sprigs parsley

FRUIT DRINK SUGGESTIONS

Melon Cocktail

Liquefy the whole melon, seeds, rind and pulp for a delicious, highly-nutritious cocktail. Melon is better used alone, but occasionally include fresh apricots, prunes, apple, peaches or pineapple for variety.

Whole Watermelon Drink

Take desired quantity of watermelon and cut into cubes, using fruit, including seeds and rind. Just a little water in the blender will start it off, and the cubes of the whole melon can be piled loosely in to fill container 3/4 full. Blend smooth. Repeat until all cubes have been blended. Strain the drink through coarse wire strainer to catch seed hulls.

Blended Fruit Drinks

1 tbsp fruit concentrate: cherry, apple or grape
1 C pineapple juice, milk, nut milk or coconut milk
Combine as desired.
Other fruits which can be added are: Bananas, blueberries, strawberries, plums, peaches, apricots, blackberries, raspberries.

Tahini Pineapple Drink

1/2 C sesame seeds or sesame butter
2 C chilled pineapple juice
A few drops lemon juice
Put sesame seeds in blender and blend until very fine. Add pineapple juice and lemon juice and blend again. Good as a bedtime sleep coaxer. Makes 3 servings.

Pineapple or Orange Yogurt Supreme

1-1/2 C yogurt   2 tbsp honey
1/2 C orange or pineapple juice
Blend all together until smooth. This is a very wholesome drink, and if desired, you can add 1 tbsp lecithin liquid, 1 tsp rice polishings. Makes 3-4 servings.

Fruit Cocktail Drink

8 oz pineapple juice   4 oz black cherry juice
1 tbsp coconut   1 tsp honey
1/4 C black walnuts   1/2 C tofu
1 banana
Blend until well liquefied. Makes 3-4 servings.

Carrot-Pineapple Supreme

1/2 C cubed celery   1/2 C cubed carrots
1-1/2 glasses chilled pineapple juice
1 tbsp lecithin granules
Blend until smooth. Makes 2 servings.

Pecan-Apple Fruit Drink

6 pecans   1 apple, diced with skin
3 tsp raisins   1 banana, peeled, quartered
1 glass pineapple juice
Put all in blender until well blended. Makes 2 servings.

Carrot-Sunflower Milk Whirl

3 C carrot juice   3/4 C sunflower seeds
Blend sunflower seeds until finely ground. Add previously-made carrot juice, blend for a few seconds. For extra nourishment, add 1 tbsp lecithin liquid when blending. Makes 4 servings.

Orange-Strawberry Delight

1 C fresh or frozen strawberries, partially thawed
1 C orange juice   2 tbsp honey
1 C ice cream or 1 C cracked ice
1 tbsp lecithin granules
Put orange juice in container, add the rest of the ingredients, and blend until smooth. Garnish with a strawberry or a piece of orange. Makes 3-4 servings.

Pineapple Sunflower Whirl

1/2 C sunflower seeds   2 C pineapple juice
1 banana, peeled and quartered
1 tbsp lecithin granules   A few drops lemon juice
Blend sunflower seeds until finely ground. Add remaining ingredients and blend until smooth. Any fruit juice can be used in place of pineapple juice. Makes 3-4 servings.

Pineapple-Grape Chiller

3 C chilled grape juice, unsweetened
1 C orange juice   2 thin slices lemon rind
2 C chilled pineapple juice, unsweetened
2 tbsp lecithin liquid
Blend all together until smooth. Makes about 7-8 servings.

Alfa-Mint Iced Tea

1 C water   1 lemon, peeled, quartered
1-inch piece lemon peel   1 tbsp honey
Put all ingredients into blender; blend well. Add to this:
1-1/2 qt hot alfa-mint tea (made as directed on package)
4-5 sprigs fresh mint (optional)
Let stand 25 min. Strain and chill until ready to serve. Honey
may be used when serving, if desired. Makes 8-10 servings.

Fresh Mint Freeze

1/2 C honey   1 C water
1 C whipped cream   1 C fresh mint leaves
1/2 C lemon juice   A little chlorophyll
                                          for color
Heat honey and water until honey is well dissolved, add mint
leaves to this and blend in blender until leaves are finely
ground. Cover and let stand until cool. Stir in lemon juice and
add green coloring. Strain into ice tray, discarding mint pulp,
and freeze until mushy. Turn into chilled bowl and beat with
electric or hand beater until smooth. Fold in whipped cream and
freeze until firm. Makes about 3 servings.

Quicky Breakfast in a Glass

1 C skim or whole milk   1 tsp honey
1 egg, raw   1/2 C any fresh fruit
1 tbsp lecithin granules   1 tbsp wheat germ flakes
1 tbsp flaxseed meal   2-3 drops lemon juice
1 tbsp sesame seed   (optional)
Blend flaxseeds, sesame seeds and lecithin granules until finely
ground. Add balance of ingredients and blend until smooth.
(This should be eaten as a food to mix with the saliva.

"Ahead of Time" Lunch Drink

Blend until finely ground:

2 tbsp sunflower, sesame seeds or almond nuts, then add:
1 C apple juice   1/2 C orange juice
1/2 C chilled, unsweetened pineapple juice
1/2 carrot, cut in small pieces   1 raw egg yolk
1 tsp raisins   1 celery stalk cut 1" pcs
2 tbsp wheat germ   1 tsp rice polishings
1 sprig parsley or watercress   2 spinach leaves
1 tbsp lecithin granules   1 C iced water
Blend all together until smooth. Serves 3-4.

Mint-Lime Drink

1 C boiling water   2 tbsp honey
1 C fresh mint leaves

Blend all together until finely ground. Chill. Strain into large
container, then add the following:
1 qt chilled water   1 C lime juice
1/4 C lemon juice
Stir until well mixed. If desired colder for serving, add an ice
cube to each glass. Serves 6-7.

Pomegranate Juice and Goat Whey

2 C liquid whey   2 lge or 3 sml
pomegranates

Extract pomegranate juice in juicer. Add to whey and serve
immediately. Makes about 3 servings.

FRUIT PUNCHES

Lemon-Mint Punch

6 sprigs fresh mint   2 C water
1 C honey   2 C lemon juice
1 qt unsweetened grape juice   Pinch sea salt
Blend mint, water and honey. Simmer 5 minutes, and strain.
Add lemon juice and salt. Chill thoroughly. Mix gently with
grape juice and serve chilled. Makes about 16-18 servings.

Pineapple-Beet "Pick-Me-Up"

2 C unsweetened pineapple juice, chilled
1 C diced raw beets
1 tbsp lecithin liquid or granules
Blend thoroughly all together in blender. If desired, add other
ingredients such as wheat germ or rice polishings. Serves 3.

Pineapple-Carrot Delight

2 C chilled pineapple juice   1 med carrot, sliced
1 orange, peeled, quartered   1 tbsp honey
1 tbsp lecithin granules or liquid
Blend until very smooth. Serve well chilled. Add chipped or
cubed ice when serving, if desired. Makes 3-4 servings.

MILK DRINKS AND FROSTED SMOOTHIES

Banana Milk

Liquefy for 1 serving:
1 C goat milk   1 ripe banana
1/2 C fruit juice   1 tbsp honey

Date Milk Drink

Blend until creamy:
5 pitted dates
1 C goat milk

1 tsp powdered coconut
1 tsp nuts

Carrot Milk

Blend until very fine and smooth:
1 C goat milk

1 med-sized carrot chopped

Banana Fig Milkshake

Blend until thick and creamy:
1/2 C thick soy milk
1/2 C fig juice
1 tsp rice polishings

1 very ripe banana
Carob to flavor, if desired

Carrot-Banana Milkshake

1/2 C milk
1 very ripe Banana

1/2 C carrot juice
1 tsp sunflower seeds

Blend until smooth and creamy. Makes 2-3 servings.

Chilly Apricot Whirl

2 C cold goat milk
3/4 C revived apricots

1 tbsp honey

Mix all ingredients in blender; chill and serve. Top with apricot half. Serves 3.

"Honey-of-a-Banana" Milkshake

1 C cold goat milk
1 banana, quartered
1 tbsp lecithin liquid

1 tbsp honey
1 C chipped ice

Blend until very smooth. This is a very healthful drink. Makes 3 servings.

Pineapple-Mint Fizz

1 C unsweetened pineapple chunks 2 C cold soy milk
  or 1 C unsweetened juice   1 sprig fresh mint
1 tbsp lecithin liquid
Blend thoroughly until nice consistency for drink. Serves 3-4.

Vanilla-Cherry Supreme

2 C red cherries or Bing cherries   1 qt cold soy milk
1 pt ice cream
Blend until real creamy. Serve in tall glasses and top with extra ice cream and a cherry.

Strawberry Milkshake Supreme

3 C chilled soy milk   2 tbsp honey
3 C fresh or frozen strawberries   1 tbsp lecithin liquid
  partially thawed   1 pt strawberry ice cream
Blend first four ingredients until thoroughly blended. Serve in glasses and top with ice cream. Serves 7-8.

Pineapple Delight

1 qt pineapple juice, unsweetened, 4 large ripe bananas
Blend together until well blended. Serves 7-8.

Cherry Whip

2 C pineapple juice   1 slice lemon or lime
1 C tart cherries or bing cherries   1 tbsp lecithin granules
Blend together until smooth. Serves 3-4.

Reducer's Special

2 C chilled unsweetened pineapple juice
1 bunch watercress   1 C crushed ice
Blend all until well blended.

Sunset Orange Glow

1 C cold soy milk

1 orange, peeled, quartered

1 tbsp honey

1/2 C orange juice

1 lemon, peeled, quartered

1 C crushed ice

Blend until smooth. Makes 2-3 servings.

Raspberry Delight

1 C fresh or frozen raspberries

2 tbsp lemon juice

2 tbsp honey

1 tbsp lecithin liquid

1-1/2 C chilled
pineapple juice

2 C chipped ice

Put pineapple juice and raspberries in blender on high. Strain to remove seeds. Return to blender and add lemon juice, honey and ice. Blend until smooth. Delightfully refreshing and a healthful drink. Serves 3-4.

"Goodnight" Snack

1 C milk

1 tbsp lecithin granules

1 tbsp molasses

Blend, then warm to comfortable drinking temperature. This helps those with sleeping problems to relax. Makes 1 serving.

Golden Daybreak Milkshake

2-3 C milk

2 tbsp honey

2 tbsp sunflower seeds

3-4 med carrots,
cut in 1" pcs

Blend sunflower seeds until finely pulverized. Add other ingredients and blend until smooth. This is a very nourishing drink for children and convalescents and can be served at any time during the day. Makes 4 servings.

Apricot Smoothie

1 C fresh soy or stewed apricots   Honey to taste
1 C soy milk   1 C cracked ice
Blend until smooth and creamy. Most other fruits can be used similarly for "smoothies" even vegetables like carrot, tomato and spinach. Soy, sesame or nut milks may be used also. Use honey, maple syrup or molasses (if any sweetening is necessary).

COCONUT MILK DRINKS

Coconut Juice or Milk

Liquefy:
1 C unsweetened shredded coconut or fresh, diced and ground dry in blender
3 C hot water
Blend half the quantity at a time if too full. Chill. Delightful addition to any milk or milk drink including soy milk.

Carrot Coconut Milk

1/2 C hot water   1 tbsp fresh coconut, grated
Liquefy and when blended add 1/2 C fresh carrot juice.

Prune Milk

1/4 C pitted prunes   1 C coconut milk or
Few drops pure vanilla   sesame milk
  or a sprinkle of cinnamon
Blend until very fine and smooth.

Mock-Choc Milk

1 heaped tbsp soy milk powder
1 tbsp honey

1/2 tbsp carob powder
1 C water

Blend until smooth and creamy.

Iced Mint Mock-Choc

3 tbsp carob sauce
1/2 tbsp honey
1/4 tsp veg broth seasoning
1/4 tsp pure vanilla
1 C cracked ice

1/2 C water
2 C thick soy milk
1 tbsp whey powder
4-5 sprigs fresh mint

Mix in blender until nice and creamy.

Mock-Choc Banana Shake

2 C soy milk or nut milk
1 banana, sliced
1 dash veg broth seasoning

1 raw egg
1/4 C carob

Blend to make smooth and creamy. Serves 2-3.

Mock-Choc Sesame Milk

1/4 C carob powder
1/3 C raw sugar

1/2 C water

Simmer 5 min, stirring occasionally. Use a good tablespoonful of this mixture to each cup sesame milk. Add a few drops of pure vanilla. Blend to a frothy drink.

THERMOS DRINKS

"Vita" Broth

1 tsp veg broth seasoning   1 C hot water
Parsley   Watercress
Other greens to suit
Blend until very smooth. Pour into preheated thermos and take to work.

Health Drink

1 tsp veg broth seasoning   1 C hot water
1 tbsp whey powder   1/4 tsp dulse
Cream to taste
Blend for a really delicious drink. Pour into preheated thermos.

Lunch in a Thermos

1 C apple or pineapple juice   2 sprigs parsley
1/2 C orange juice   1 tsp raisins
2 spinach or Romaine leaves   3/4 C cashews or almonds
1/2 C fresh fruit   1 sml celery stalk, diced
1 sml piece banana   1 raw egg
1/2 C carrots, diced   2 tsp wheat germ
1 tsp rice polishings
Blend all ingredients for 3 minutes. Add 1 C crushed ice and pour into thermos. This makes a complete meal.

PROTEIN AND STARCH DRINKS

Protein Drink One

1 C buttermilk   1 egg yolk
1 tsp brewer's yeast   2 tbsp wheat germ
1 tsp veg broth seasoning   1 tbsp gelatin
Few drops lemon juice

Protein Drink Two

1 C papaya tea	3 tbsp sunflower seeds
4 tbsp cottage cheese	4 dates

Protein Drink Three

1 C goat milk	2 tbsp skim milk powder
1 tsp rice polishings	1/4 tsp dulse
1 tbsp black walnut butter	1/3 tsp molasses
3 apricots	

Protein Drink Four
Hot Mock-Choc

2 tbsp carob powder	3/4 C hot nut milk
2 tbsp skim milk powder	

Special Protein Cocktail

1 C cold goat milk	1 egg yolk
1/2 cheddar cheese, diced	1 tbsp flaxseed
1 tbsp lecithin granules	1 tbsp wheat germ
1 tbsp rice polishings	

Put flaxseed in blender and blend finely. Add rest of ingredients and blend until smooth. This makes a delicious-tasting and nourishing protein snack. Serves 2-3. Dr. Jensen believes in Raw goat's milk.

LIQUEFIED DRINKS

These drinks are very tasty and nutritious. Try serving them to your drop-in guests.

Drink #1
(Serves 3-4)

1 C black cherry juice
2 C unsweetened pineapple juice
2 tbsp soy powder
1 tbsp wheat germ

2 tbsp honey
1 banana
1 egg yolk
1 tsp rice polishings

Drink #2

1 banana
1/2 C chopped parsley
2 tbsp honey

2 tbsp soy powder
1 C papaya juice

Drink #3
(Serves 3)

1 C blackberry juice
1 C pineapple juice and
  crushed pineapple
1 tbsp honey

1 banana
1 egg yolk
2 tbsp soy powder

Blend together and serve with shredded coconut.

OTHER DRINKS

#1

1 C soy milk
1/4 tsp dulse
Few drops vanilla or lemon

4 tbsp cooked cereal
Honey to taste

#2

1 C carrot juice
Piece of celery

1/2 C corn, off cob
Veg broth seasoning

After blending this can be sieved. Add a little sweet raw cream.

Note. Sweet potatoes or yams also make a very good base for drinks.

Lima Bean Drink

3 tbsp veg broth powder   1 C cooked lima beans
1 tbsp brewer's yeast   1 tbsp whey powder
1 tbsp honey
Blend together until smooth. Add 2 tbsp cream and blend a few seconds longer. Season to taste. Serve warm or cold. Serves 3.

NUT AND SEED DRINKS

The blender will chop nuts in 3 to 5 seconds, grind them to a powder in a little more time or reduce them to a butter. Quick switches to on and off at high speed, and a rubber scraper to scrape off the sides accomplish this. The longer you blend, the finer the butter.

By using a liquid with your nuts and seeds, you can whip nutritious milk-substitute drinks in no time. Liquefied nuts can be handled very nicely in the intestinal tract.

Almond Nut Milk

Use blanched or unblanched almonds (or other nuts). Soak overnight in pineapple juice, apple juice or honey water. This softens the nut meats. Then put 3 ounces of soaked nuts into 5 ounces of water and blend for 2-3 minutes. Flavor with honey, any kind of fruit: strawberry juice, carob flour, dates or bananas. Any of the vegetable juices are also good with nut milks.

Nut milks can also be used with soups and vegetarian roasts as a flavoring or over cereals. Almond milk makes a very alkaline drink, high in protein and easy to assimilate and absorb.

Seeds and Sprouts

Seeds and sprouts are going to be the foods of the future. We have found that many of the seeds have the hormone values of male and female glands. Seeds carry the life force for many years, as long as they are enclosed by the hull. Seeds found in Egyptian tombs known to be thousands of years old, have grown when planted. To get these seeds into our bodies in the form of a drink, gives us the finest nutrition.

Flaxseed and sunflower seeds, sesame seeds, apricot kernels, dry melon seeds, etc., grind dry in the liquefier very well. As these deteriorate quickly, keep your blender handy and grind them as often as needed. Don't store the dry ground seeds or they will go rancid.

Cantaloupe Seed Drink

Instead of throwing away the seeds and pulp from the inside of the cantaloupe, blend these thoroughly with a little pineapple juice or oat straw tea, sweetened with honey; strain to remove the seed hulls, and serve as a delicious "nut" milk drink, rich in the vital elements of seeds.

Variation. **Squash seeds** may be similarly treated in a suitable liquid, flavored with honey or maple syrup and a few dates or sliced fresh fruit.

Sesame Seed Milk

I believe that sesame seed milk is one of our best. It is a wonderful drink for gaining weight and for lubricating the intestinal tract. Its nutritional value is beyond compare, as it is high in protein and minerals. This is the seed that is used so much as a basic food in Arabia and East India.

Blend 2 C water, 1/4 C sesame seed, 2 tbsp soy milk powder; blend until smooth. Strain if desired through a fine-wire strainer or three or four layers of cheesecloth. This removes the hulls. (Hulless sesame seeds can be used.)

Variation. 1 tbsp carob powder and 6 to 8 dates. Blend in for flavor and added nutritional value any one of the following: Banana, date powder, stewed raisins or grape sugar. After any addition, always blend to mix. This drink can also be made from goat's milk in place of the water.

Other Uses for Sesame Seed Milk

Salad dressing base, add to fruits, after-school snacks, add to vegetable broth, use on cereals for breakfast, mix with any nut butter, take twice daily with bananas to gain weight, add to whey drinks to adjust intestinal sluggishness and with supplements such as flaxseed or rice polishings.

Sunflower Seed Milk

The same principle used for making nut milks can be employed to make sunflower seed milk; i.e., soaking overnight, liquefying and flavoring with fruits and juices. Use in the diet the same as almond nut milk. It is best to use whole sunflower seeds and blend them yourself. If you do not have a liquefier, sunflower seed meal can be used.

Soy Milk and Soy Cream

Soy milk power is available in every health food store.

For soy milk, add 2 tbsp of soy milk powder to one pint of water. Sweeten with raw sugar, honey or molasses and add a pinch of vegetable seasoning. For flavor, you can add any kind of fruit, carob powder, dates and bananas.

Keep in refrigerator. Use this milk in any recipe as you would regular cow's milk. It closely resembles the taste and composition of cow's milk and will sour just as quickly, so it should not be made too far ahead of time.

NUT DRINKS

Teas can be substituted for water in the following drinks; e.g., oat straw tea, strawberry tea, peach-leaf tea and golden seal tea.

Nut Cream or Nut Milk

Soak seeds or nuts overnight. Do not wash after soaking. Excellent choices are almonds (blanched after soaking if desired), sunflower seeds, sesame seeds or any other nuts.

1-1/4 C soaked seeds or nuts   1 C pure water
Liquefy and blend well.
Add and blend well:
2 tbsp honey   2 tbsp sesame oil
Veg broth seasoning (optional)

For Nut Milk, add more water. Refrigerate. This keeps several days.

Maple Nut Fruit Nectar

1 tsp pure maple syrup   3 tbsp raw nuts
1 C fruit juice

Maple Nut Banana Cream

1 tbsp maple syrup   2 tbsp nuts
1 C milk   1 tbsp sweet raw cream
1 ripe banana, sliced
Blend nice and creamy. Serve cold or warm.

Jumbo Fruit/Nut Drink
(Serves 3-4)

1 C pineapple juice
1/2 C black cherry juice
2 tbsp soy milk powder
1 tbsp coconut
6 pitted dates

1 tbsp honey
1/4 C black walnuts
1 egg
1 sliced banana

Pecan-Apple Fruit Drink

Blend:
6 pecans, soaked
1 apple, diced
3 tsp raisins

1 banana, sliced
1 C pineapple juice

SESAME SEED SUGGESTIONS

Sesame-Banana Milkshake

1 C sesame milk
3-4 chopped, pitted dates

1 sliced banana

Sesame Fruit Shake

1 C sesame seed milk
2-3 chopped dates

1/2 banana, chopped
Small slice papaya

Sesame Supplement Cream

Blend well and use on breakfast cereal or over fruit:
1 C sesame milk
1 tsp flaxseed meal
3-4 dates, chopped, or raisins,
  figs or papaya

1 tsp rice polishings
1 tbsp sunflower seed meal
1 tbsp wheat germ

Sesame Nut Cream

1 C sesame milk   1/2 C nut butter
  or 1 tsp sesame seed butter   6 pitted dates, chopped
Any juice (w/sesame seed butter)
Blend well and serve over breakfast fruit or use as a sweet
dressing for salads.

Sesame Seed Dressing

1 C boiling water   1 C sesame seed or meal
1 C cold-pressed oil   4 tbsp veg broth seasoning
Lemon juice to taste
Blend the sesame in the water smooth first, then add the oil,
seasoning and lemon juice and blend to make a thick, creamy
dressing. Thin or change to suit taste.

Dr. Jensen's Drink

1 tbsp sesame seed meal or butter   1/4 avocado
1 tsp honey
1 glass liquid (fruit juice, vegetable juice, soy milk or broth and
water)
Blend half a minute.

NATURAL REMEDIES AND TONICS

It is best not to use a remedy for a specific condition unless
your whole diet is nutritionally balanced. Eating atrocious foods
and trying to find a remedy for conditions you are producing
doesn't make good sense. Use my Health and Harmony Food
Regimen as a guide for a nutritionally-balanced diet.

Alkalinizing System

Liquefy:
1/2 C grapefruit   1/4 C pineapple juice
Few spinach leaves

Appetite

Liquefy:
3/4 C pineapple juice   Dandelion leaves

Arthritis

Alfalfa seed tea: Put 1 tbsp alfalfa seeds in 1 pt water. Bring to boil and let set overnight. Strain and drink liquid.

Blood Builders
No. 1

1 C mixed celery, parsley, spinach 1 C desired veg juice base
1 C bing cherry juice

No. 2

1 C cherry, grape or pineapple juice   1 tbsp whey powder
1 dulse tablet or   1 egg yolk
  1/4 tsp dulse powder

Body Builder

1/2 C coconut milk   3 fresh or revived dried figs
Liquefy.

Brain and Nervous System

Liquefy protein drinks, especially with raw whole egg or egg yolk, or a hard, unprocessed cheese, cottage cheese, sunflower seeds, soaked nuts, wheat germ, rice bran or polishings, 2-3 tsp daily. (Papaya tea as a base aids protein digestion.)

Radish, prune juice and rice polishings for nervous disorders.

Celery, carrot and prune juice for nervous tension.

Lettuce and tomato juices for a nerve quieter.

Complexion
No. 1

Liquefy:

1 tbsp apple concentrate   1/2 C water
1/2 cucumber

No. 2

Cucumber juice, pineapple juice and endive. Liquefy.

Coronary (Heart)

Any sweet, sweetened or carbohydrate drinks; e.g., carrot, pineapple juice and honey.

One tsp honey in glass of water three times daily (in lieu of other sweets).

Diarrhea

Try carob powder to control.

Gastro-Intestinal

Use any combination of vegetables. Sieve after liquefying.
(Various stomach and intestinal disorders cannot tolerate fibrous
material.)
Liquefy, then strain:
1 C tomato juice   1 stalk celery
Few leaves of watercress or endive

Whey: Use whey in any milk or liquefied drink for intestinal
management. It is high in sodium. It may be used plain as a
drink or in combination with a wide variety of foods, especially
in liquefied drinks.

Carrot juice and coconut milk (for colitis, gastritis and gas).

An aid in ulcer conditions is egg white, beaten to a stiff froth,
and used as a topping on liquefied drinks.

Gland and Nerve

1 C sweet cherry juice   1 tsp chlorophyll
1 egg yolk   2 tbsp wheat germ
Blend in liquefier.

Hair (for sheen)

1 C sweet cherry juice   1 C oat straw tea

Kidneys

Parsley tablets; blend into drinks.

Laxative

Prune juice   Yellow fruits, vegetables
Drink a warm cup of herb tea first thing in morning.

Respiratory-Catarrhal

Foods high in vitamins A and C: Bell peppers (especially ripe ones) have high content of vitamin C. Parsley is in vitamin A. Use as a base juice or ingredient in liquefied drinks; e.g., tomato juice and green peppers liquefied.

Rheumatic

Whey: Use whey with cherry juice, with any broth, soup, milk or liquefied drink.

Foods high in vitamin C and sodium hold calcium in solution to maintain suppleness in joints; e.g., tomato juice and celery juice.

Skin

Liquefy:
1/2 C pineapple juice   1/3 chopped cucumber
Sprigs of parsley

Oat straw tea and rice polishings.

Vitality

Liquefy:
1 C apple juice   1 tbsp almond nut butter
1 C celery juice   Soy milk powder
Wheat germ

Weight Gaining

Liquefy:
Dried fruit, revived   Pineapple juice
Soy milk   Nut butters

Flaxseed tea (liquefied if you wish to use the seed) added to any liquefied fruit or protein drink, can be weight gaining.

Weight Reducing

Liquefied protein drinks; e.g., for a satisfying noon meal: Cottage cheese in soy milk or whey, with apricot or peach nectar, apple juice for flavor.

Use fresh fruits in preference to dried. Fresh apples are wonderful liquefied; e.g., diced apple in pineapple juice.

Good bases are tomato, papaya or pineapple juices. For a citrus base, use grapefruit pulp liquefied (after removing the peel and dicing); liquefied sections of orange with pulp.

Nut and Seed Milks (see recipes).

Soybean milk may be made with low-fat soybean powder, obtainable at health food stores.

Example: Soy bean milk   1 egg yolk
Honey   Fresh strawberries
Liquefy. (Other fresh fruits or juices may be used.)

Try watercress tablets liquefied in drinks.

Use Gelatin Whey:
1/4 C cold water   2 tbsp plain gelatin
Blend the two then add: 3/4 C boiling water and blend; 3 tbsp whey powder, and blend.
Variations:
Vanilla: add a few drops of pure vanilla.
Orange: add 1 tbsp orange juice and a little grated rind.
Mint: use mint tea instead of water.

JUICE AND BLENDER COMBINATIONS
FOR AILMENTS

For: **Use:**

Anemia: Parsley, grape juice
Asthma: Celery, papaya juice
Bed-Wetting: Celery, parsley juice
Bladder ailments: Celery, pomegranate juice
Catarrh, colds, sore throat: Watercress, apple juice
                                            (add 1/4 tsp cream of tartar)
Constipation,
stomach ulcers: Celery with a little sweet cream,
                                            spinach and grapefruit juice.
Colds, sinus trouble: Celery and grapefruit juices
                                            (add 1/4 tsp cream of tartar)
Diarrhea, infection: Carrot and blackberry juice
Fever, gout, arthritis: Celery and parsley juice
Gallbladder disorders: Radish, prune, black cherry and
                                            celery juice
General housecleaning: Celery, parsley, spinach and
                                            carrot juice
Glands, goiter, impotence: Celery juice, 1 tsp wheat germ,
                                            1/2 tsp Nova Scotia dulse
High blood pressure: Carrot, parsley, celery juice
Indigestion, underweight: Coconut milk, fig, parsley and
                                            carrot juice
Insomnia, sleeplessness: Lettuce and celery juice
Kidney disorders: Celery, parsley, asparagus juice
Liver disorders: Radish and pineapple juices
Neuralgia: Cucumber, endive, pineapple juice
Overweight, obesity: Beet greens, parsley, celery juice
Poor circulation: Beet and blackberry juice
Poor memory: Celery, carrot, prune juice and
                                            rice polishings
Poor teeth: Beet greens, parsley, celery juice
                                            and green kale

For:	Use:
Reducing:	Parsley, grape juice, pineapple juice
Rheumatism, neuritis, neuralgia:	Cucumber, endive and whey
Rickets:	Dandelion and orange juice
Scurvy, eczema:	Carrot, celery, lemon juice

CHAPTER NINE

HOW JUICE FITS IN THE BIG PICTURE

I believe juices are the finest supplements we can take to make sure we are getting all the vitamins, minerals and enzymes needed (and perhaps just a little extra) to take care of our constitutionally-weak organs and tissues, our immune systems and all the vital functions of the body. Juices are wonderful! But, except for an occasional doctor-supervised juice fast, juices must be part of a whole, pure and natural diet. The human body wasn't meant to thrive on liquids alone, so now we will consider my Health and Harmony Food Regimen, which was designed to fit the nutritional needs of the great majority of people.

This food regimen, which I developed over the years of my sanitarium work, is designed to give you principles and guidelines that allow you to take responsibility for the actual food selection. On my Ranch, the cooks chose the foods under my supervision. But, in your house, you will be responsible for choosing the foods. Over the years, I've had the pleasure of seeing many patients grow out of their symptoms just by restoring the chemical balance in their bodies through right nutrition and right living.

DR. JENSEN'S HEALTH AND HARMONY
FOOD REGIMEN

Rules of Eating

1. **Do not fry foods or use heated oils in cooking.** Frying lowers nutritional value, destroys lecithin needed to balance fats and makes food harder to digest. The temperature at which foods are fried or cooked in oil alters food chemistry, which is not a safe practice. This can be one of the greatest contributing factors to cholesterol formation and hardening of the arteries and heart disease.

2. **If not entirely comfortable in mind and body, do not eat.** We don't digest food well when we are upset or when we are not comfortable. A little waiting period from food will allow us to digest our food properly.

3. **Do not eat until you have a keen desire for the plainest food.** Too often, we eat simply because it's mealtime, not because we are hungry. Break this undesirable habit. To have the best possible digestion, eat when you are hungry.

4. **Do not eat beyond your needs.** Overeating is not good for your health.

5. **Be sure to thoroughly masticate your food.** Chewing well increases the efficiency of digestion. You get more food value for the money you spend on food.

6. **Miss meals if in pain, emotionally upset, not hungry, chilled, overheated or ill.** Each of these conditions is a signal that we need rest, warmth, calmness or something other than food, which, if eaten, ties up considerable energy and blood in the gastrointestinal tract. Often, rest is the thing most needed. Food takes energy to digest and involves work by several organs, and it may take hours before food energy is available.

Rules for Getting Well

1. Learn to accept whatever decision is made. Do your best to keep your peace of mind. Peace is a healer.

2. Let the other person make a mistake and learn. This is so much better than standing over people and supervising every move. Learn to give the person the opportunity to grow and grow up. We are bound to make mistakes. Let's not gloat over them and live in remorse about them.

3. Learn to forgive and forget. Many studies have now shown that forgiving enhances health and helps prevent chemical changes in the body that may lead to disease.

4. Be thankful and bless people. These are two of the main secrets to a healthy live.

5. Live in harmony—even if it is good for you.

6. Don't talk about your misfortunes or illnesses. It doesn't do any good for you or the person you tell, and it presents an opportunity for them to do the same to you. Save it for your doctor. He's paid to listen to your troubles.

7. Don't gossip. Gossip that comes through the grapevine is usually sour grapes.

8. Spend 10 minutes a day meditating on how you can become a better person. Replace negative thoughts with positive ones.

9. Exercise daily. Keep your spine and joints limber, develop your abdominal muscles, expand your lungs—with specific exercises on a regular schedule.

10. Walk 10 minutes barefoot in the dewy grass or sand the first thin in the morning to stimulate the blood circulation.

11. No smoking or drinking of alcohol. Both nicotine and alcohol are depressant drugs. Both require energy to detoxify the body which is needed for more useful life processes.

12. Go to bed by 9 pm, at the latest, when you can. If you are tired during the day, rest. Rest allows the body to give its full attention and energy to healing and rebuilding tissues. Write down your problems at the end of the day and go over them first thing in the morning when you are refreshed, so you can look at them with a fresh mind and body.

Total Healing Laws

Food is for building health. You need to have foods that will meet the needs of a vital, active life and the following laws are designed to do exactly that. These are physical laws to be carried out. Try to understand what it means to get your diet program working out according to these laws.

1. Food should be natural, whole, pure and fresh. Reason: **The closer food is to its natural, God-created state, the higher its nutritional value.** Some foods, such as meat, potatoes, yams and grains must be cooked. Whole foods are more nutritious than refined, bleached or peeled foods. I'm not telling you to eat banana skins and avocado seeds, I'm just giving you a practical guideline. Pure foods are much better for us than foods with preservatives, artificial colors or flavors or chemical additives of any kind. Many chemicals now added to commercial food products were never meant to be in the human body. Our bodies were designed for natural, whole, pure, fresh foods and that's what keeps us in the best condition. We have learned our greatest lesson with experiments on animals using denatured, peeled, polished foods. They have become sick because the biochemicals have been deleted and they are no longer whole, as God designed them for us.

2. We should have 60% of our foods raw. Reason: **I am not advising a raw diet because I like the taste, I'm saying it is better for us.** Raw foods provide more vitamins, minerals, enzymes, fiber and bulk, because they are "live" foods at the peak of nutritional value, if properly selected. Raw foods help the digestive system and bowel. I mean fruits, berries, vegetables, sprouts, nuts and seeds. We have to cook cereal grains, lima beans, artichokes and other foods, but there are many we can take raw.

3. We should have 6 vegetables, 2 fruits, 1 starch and 1 protein every day. Reason: **Vegetables are high in fiber and minerals. Fruits are high in natural complex sugars and vitamins.** Starch is for energy and protein is for cell repairing and rebuilding, especially the brain and nerves. **This is a balanced combination of foods.**

4. Our foods should be 80% alkaline and 20% acid. Reason: **We find that 80% of the nutrients carried in the blood are alkaline and 20% are acid. To keep the blood the way it should be, 6 vegetables and 2 fruits make up that 80% alkaline foods we need, while 1 protein and 1 starch make up the 20% of acid foods.** To keep the blood balanced, we should eat 2 fruits, 6 vegetables, 1 starch and 1 protein daily. Proteins and many starches are acid-forming and nearly all the metabolic wastes of the body are acids. We need alkaline-forming foods such as fruit and vegetables so their alkaline salts will neutralize the acid wastes. I believe that we should recognize that to keep the proper alkaline-acid balance in the body we must have 6 vegetables, 2 fruits, 1 starch and 1 protein daily. There is no reason why we should add too heavily to the acid conditions in our body by adding heavy acid foods such as we find in the proteins and starches. In my experience, acid wastes not properly disposed of are the cause of many disturbances, health problems and chronic diseases.

5. Variety: Vary proteins, starches, vegetables and fruits from meal to meal and day to day. Reason: **Every organ of our body needs one chemical element more than others to keep healthy.** The thyroid needs iodine, the stomach needs sodium, the blood needs iron and so on. We also need variety in vitamins. The best way to take care of this is to have variety in vitamins. The best way to take care of this is to have variety in our foods. Foods, in a way, are matched to our body organs in that each food is usually highest in one or two minerals and vitamins. But every food is different and even the same foods grown in different localities, different soils, have different nutrients. As we take in a variety of foods, we must realize that we are made from the dust of the earth. To get calcium foods, we need grains and different kinds of grains. Some grains have more calcium than other grains. It is necessary to realize that in our variety, especially our salads, they must be made up of different colors. Each color has its own activity in the body, because each color carries a chemical element particular to that color. All red foods are stimulating foods. All yellow are of a laxative nature in the natural food routine. All green foods repair, rebuild and are high in iron and potassium. For example, a rainbow salad will have all the chemical elements we need in the various colors of vegetables. The same applies to the main dish. If you can follow this reasoning and go into it deeper and see how each chemical element has its own vibration, each color found in the foods has its own vibration. We are eating the life force, the sun-giving force from these fruits and vegetables in the color that was placed there by nature. This is one of the greatest laws to follow.

6. Eat moderately. Reason: **The healthiest people I have met in my world travels were the same weight later in life as when they were in their 20s, and some of them were over 120 years of age!** In the U.S., 60% of the people are overweight, which leads to many health problems. Leave that extra food on the plate. Eating at home is more desirable. **The bigger the waistline, the shorter the lifeline.**

7. Combinations: Separate starches and proteins. Reason: **Have your proteins and starches at different meals, not because they don't digest well together, but so you will be able to eat more fruits and vegetables each meal.** People tend to fill up on protein and starch, then neglect their vegetables. I want you to have a lot of vegetables with each meal for your health's sake, and when you are hungry, they taste wonderful. There are poor combinations, and I'll mention a few. Dried fruits do not go well with fresh fruits. Unless dried fruits have been reconstituted and brought back to their natural state, it is best not to eat them. It is best not to have grapefruit and dates together. Dried fruits must be reconstituted by putting the dried fruit in cold water at night and bring them to a boil, let the water boil for about 3 minutes, then turn off the flame; let stand overnight. Melon should always be eaten at least half an hour apart from any other foods.

Don't have ice-cold drinks with meals because they interfere with digestion. Herb teas can be taken with meals and so can vegetable or fruit juices, since they are foods. There is a lot of discussion about having liquids with meals. It is best to have your fruit at breakfast and 3 pm.

8. Be careful about your drinking water. Reason: **Most public water systems are now highly chemicalized because ground water sources are increasingly polluted.** The fruit and vegetables in my Health and Harmony Food Regimen supply much of the water your body needs. If you use broths, juices, soups and herbal teas, they will take care of any remaining thirst during the day. If you are still thirsty, try cutting down or eliminating salt on your foods. Salt creates a thirst. Use vegetable or broth seasonings instead. I advise distilled water for those who have arthritis but we don't really need much drinking water on my Health and Harmony Food Regimen. Reverse osmosis water purification units provide the best water for household consumption.

9. Use low-heat, waterless cookware; cook with little or no water and do not overcook. Reason: **High heat, boiling in water and exposure to air are the three greatest robbers of nutrients.** Low-heat stainless steel pots with lids that form a water seal are the most efficient means of cooking foods in such a way as to preserve the greatest nutritional value. For oven cooking, glass casserole dishes with lids are fine. I approve of crockpot cooking, because it offers another low-heat method.

10. If you use meat, poultry and fish, bake, broil or roast it—but have it no more than 3 times a week. Reason: **Baking, broiling and roasting—while far from perfect cooking methods—are at least more acceptable in terms of preserving more nutritional value. Cook at lower heats for longer times to retain the most nutritional value.** Avoid pork and fatty meats and use only white fish with fins and scales. Salmon is permitted, even though it isn't a white meat. Fatty meats lead to obesity, heart trouble and so on. Beef is very stimulating to the heart and I do not recommend using it. Eating meat more than three times a week can produce excess uric acid and other irritating by-products causing an unnecessary burden on the body. While I do not believe that the meat will cause heart trouble, I believe when we live a fast, hard lifestyle that includes having a heavy amount of meat, it can lead to heart troubles. Those who study the positive and negative effects of food will find that meat is positive, starches are negative.

Starches feed the left side of the body, and that is the side where the heart is. Proteins feed the right side of the body.

11. Avoid having an excess of one or a few foods in the diet. Reason: **An excess of one or a few foods may provide too much of certain food chemicals for the body to handle, causing irritation, inflammation or possible allergies.** Celiac disease is caused by gluten from wheat and other gluten grains damage the wall of the small bowel. An excess of one or a few foods also means that other foods are not used in sufficient variety in the diet, which causes chemical deficiencies.

12. Don't neglect important foods. Reason: **Our health is determined as much by what we don't eat as well as by what we eat, which can cause nutritional deficiencies that lead to a future disease.** If we neglect most vegetables, for example, we prevent our bodies from receiving needed chemical elements and enzymes. Lack of sufficient proteins, carbohydrates and fats—any or all—can cause disturbances in the body, as can lack of vitamins, minerals, lecithin, enzymes and trace elements.

Daily Eating Regimen

Organize your meals to use the food laws and instructions properly. Here is an outline of what your daily food regimen should be like, and this will take care of the food laws—the law of variety, the law of proportions, the law of acid/alkaline balance, the law of 60% raw food and so forth.

You can have half your daily allowance of protein at breakfast and half at dinner; half of your starch at breakfast and half at lunch. Starches and proteins together help keep you from snacking and experiencing hunger between meals, but you shouldn't have so much that you don't have room for vegetables.

Breakfast: 1/2 starch, 1/2 protein, health drink.

10 am: Vegetable juice or broth.

Lunch: 3 vegetables (cooked, raw or salad), 1/2 starch, health drink.

3 pm: Fruit or fruit juice

Dinner: 3 vegetables (cooked, raw or salad), 1/2 protein, health drink.

Before Breakfast

It is best to have a couple of glasses of water or a drink of some kind before breakfast. This cleanses the bladder and kidneys. I have found the practice of taking a teaspoon of liquid chlorophyll in a glass of water is one of the best things to start the day off. I avoid citrus juices in the morning, as they stir up acids. Remember citrus stirs up acids, while vegetable juices carry them off. Other juices you might have could be a glass of natural, unsweetened fruit juice: grape, pineapple, prune, fig, apple or black cherry.

Breakfast

Fruit, one starch and a health drink (broth, soup, coffee substitute, buttermilk, raw milk, oat straw tea, alfa-mint tea, huckleberry tea, papaya tea, etc.). Dried, unsulfured fruits should be reconstituted. Fresh fruit such as melon, grapes, apricots, figs, pears, berries, apple slices (or baked apple) may be sprinkled with ground nuts, seeds or nut butter. Ground sesame seeds, flax seeds, sunflower seeds and almonds are good. Try to use fruit in season. If you have a cooked whole grain cereal, sprinkle ground nuts and seeds on top, add chopped dates, raisins, prunes, figs or other dried fruit for sweetening or use a little honey or maple syrup. A handful of steamed raisins in any cereal has been a favorite with our family. We can use Swiss muesli any time. Avoid citrus or citrus juices with breakfast, except an occasional ripe orange, sliced in sections.

Lunch

Raw salad: tomatoes, lettuce (no head lettuce), celery, cucumber, spinach leaves, sprouts (bean, alfalfa, radish, etc.), green pepper, avocado, parsley, watercress, endive, onion, garlic, cabbage, cauliflower, broccoli, etc., in any combination. Top with grated carrot, beet, parsnip, turnip, in any combination. Sprinkle with ground nuts and seeds. Add a little grated cheese, if you like. One or two starches may be used, plus a health drink.

Dinner

Protein, vegetable or fruit salad, one or two cooked vegetables (such as squash, artichoke, cauliflower, spinach, chard, Brussels sprouts, broccoli, etc.) and a health drink. If you had a large salad for lunch, have a small one for dinner and *vice versa.*

Desserts

I do not believe in desserts, however, we find occasionally many people have to have it, so here are some suggestions. We can have a sliced apple, raw fruit salad, mixture of cut-up apples and steamed raisins with maple syrup. Mix gelatin with cherry juice and put a little whipped cream on it. Or why not have a banana, apple, pear or apricot? There are homemade candies, and one is made with nut butter and dried fruits, rolled in coconut.

Suggestions for Preparing
Breakfast, Lunch and Dinner

Breakfast. In many countries, breakfast is considered the main meal because most people believe a good breakfast is necessary to get them going. They believe they have to have something in their bodies to get every organ stimulated and working. They think that in that stimulated condition, they are ready for work. However, the strength and power to work with is in the tissues. The strength we have in the morning comes from our meal at noon the day before. After eating food, it takes some 18 hours before it gets to the tissues to give strength to our bodies. Once the "response" part of the body—the nervous system—is fed and repaired, we have the strength to work. The food we eat at noon today will give us our energy tomorrow afternoon. But what we eat for breakfast will be reacting tonight, when we go to bed. This is not the time we should be stimulated. This is one reason why we should have a light breakfast. We don't want to be ready to go to work at night when it is bedtime. We should have our heavy meal at noon. The strength derived from that comes just in time to start our day right the following morning.

Preparing Whole Grains Cereals. The best way is to use a wide-mouth thermos. Put the cereal grain into the bottle, cover with boiling water and let soak overnight. Make sure there's room for the cereal to expand without breaking the thermos. Exception: Cornmeal must always be added to cold water and brought to a boil in a pan first or it lumps. When it has boiled, pour the mixture into a thermos and leave overnight. Cereal can also be cooked in a double boiler.

Ground Nuts and Seeds. You can grind several types of nuts and seeds in advance and keep them in small jars or plastic containers in the refrigerator. Bring them out at mealtimes. You can sprinkle these on fruits, vegetables, salads, cereals, baked potato, almost any food.

Other Supplements. You can add psyllium husks, wheat bran, wheat germ, oat bran, flax seed meal, dulse or broth powder seasoning on many foods to add fiber, flavor and nutritional value. Herbs are a fine addition.

The main thing we are trying to bring out in our diet work is **what is right** for a person and not **who** is right. There must be some regular or definite program that fits most people. The word "breakfast" comes from the root break fast. Whenever we fast or go without food, all night long digestive juices flow slower, our whole body is working slower; therefore, when we wake, we should break the fast with a fruit juice or a light nourishing drink of some kind. Then we should have a fruit breakfast. Fruit is the proper thing to break a fast. If we like, a little protein is a good combination with fruit and it may be allowed. We can also have dried fruits and carbohydrates together for breakfast. The idea of having fried foods, a lot of muffins, bread or French toast, and all the other heavy foods is not right. It is not a matter of seeing how much we can eat.

Lunch

If you want energy for the next morning, eat a good lunch. That "washed-out" feeling with which so many housewives start the day is probably due to the fact that they can't always be bothered to fix a nourishing meal for themselves at midday. They may fix a sandwich with white break and a filling with no nutritional value, and a cup of coffee.

We will follow along with the starch idea at noon because most people are in the habit of having sandwiches or break for this meal. Make sure your sandwiches are made of thinly-sliced whole grain breads, and stuffed heartily with good fillings and plenty of vegetables to aid the digestion. Avocado, grated carrot, celery and nuts, cottage cheese and alfalfa sprouts, olives and lettuce, nuts and dates, sunflower seed meal and honey are a few suggestions. Use a spoonful of health mayonnaise, cream or mashed banana to stick them together. Flavor with vegetable seasonings and dulse. Along with your sandwiches, take extra salad ingredients such as green leaves, carrot and celery sticks, green peppers, cucumbers or tomatoes. A health cookie is permissible, but wouldn't a bag of nuts, sunflower or squash seeds, raisins, dates or figs be more pleasing?

Did you know you can make sandwiches without bread? Bread is not the only starch, in fact, it is one of the least desirable, and even if you pack a lunch, other starches are easily possible. Slice an apple horizontally and wedge cheese between the slices for instance. Raw baby zucchini slices make a nice "bread" to stuff with nut butter; some people use raw eggplant sliced thin and filled with a tasty mayonnaise spread. Even lettuce leaves will sandwich together many lovely fillings.

Starches: Yellow cornmeal, baked potato, ripe or baked banana, yam, sweet potato, barley, rye, millet, brown rice, wild rice (actually this is a seed), buckwheat, squash such as banana, acorn or spaghetti. A couple of dead-ripe bananas can become the hub of your lunch. Never forget variety. These can be quite easily be put in a thermos if you have to carry your lunch. A thermos has many uses. It can hold your cold fruit or vegetable cocktail in summer, your hot broth or herb tea in winter. It can also hold a cool fruit whip or soy or nut milk beverages.

Lunch time is salad time. You will be on the move again shortly, and it takes exercise to handle raw food. Have your big green, raw salad at noon, using as many vegetables as possible. It is amazing the number we can use raw such as summer squash, asparagus, Jerusalem artichokes, okra, cauliflower and turnips, to mention just a few of the more unusual. These can be extremely tasty grated and occasionally dressed with a tangy mayonnaise. For eye appeal, sometimes stuff a green pepper, tomato or celery sticks. (These can even be carried to work in a jar. So can salads, although they lose value if left cut up too long. It is best to take vegetables along whole.)

Have a cooked, low-starch-type vegetable with your meal, too, if you like. When serving a root vegetable, always make sure you have a "top" vegetable with it—not necessarily the matching top or green. On colder days, a nourishing soup is welcome. And why not try a cool, raw soup in summer?

Finish your meal with a health drink: herb tea, dandelion coffee, buttermilk, raw milk, whey or any good health beverage.

It really doesn't take so very long to prepare a lunch such as we suggested, and the lift it will give your vitality and good humor will be well worth it.

Dinner

If you value your health, eat at home! No one suffers more from malnutrition than the clergyman's wife, who is always out to supper, attending a church luncheon or supervising the Sunday school.

Dinner should be a family affair, a happy get-together at the end of the day when news can be exchanged convivially at the family dinner table. Here, children can learn by example the rules of healthy eating, a happy attitude, quiet enjoyment, manners, cultivation of a desire for plain food, eating slowly and masticating, and most important, knowing when to stop eating.

Use the evening meal to balance your day nutritionally. If you skimped on your salad at noon, have a bigger one at dinner or begin the meal with a raw vegetable cocktail. Did you get your quota of two fruits today? Have a fruit dessert or Waldorf salad for dinner. A mixed vegetable broth is an excellent way to bring up your vegetable intake for the day—there are very good recipes for raw soups, too/

Plan your dinner around this basic formula: A small raw salad, 2 cooked vegetables, 1 protein and a health drink. If you are not a vegetarian, have meat two or three times a week, but make sure it is lean meat and cooked by broiling or roasting without fat. Fish once a week is a good protein high in iodine and phosphorus. Choose fish with fins and scales and steam, grill or bake it. Two nights a week serve a cheese dish. You'll find a popular summer supper is plain cheeses with fruit. Cheese that breaks or cottage cheese and a variety of fruit make a complete meal. An egg dish, such as a souffle or omelet, plain, poached or scrambled eggs on spinach or other greens can complete the week's dinners. There are all the vegetable proteins to bring in the changes. Nuts are one of our high-protein foods. The almond is king. Always soak nuts for several hours in fruit juice, tea or honey water for better digestion. Nuts are best eaten raw. A good form is as a nut butter. Beans baked or in roasts, lentils, split peas and sunflower seeds can also be used. An excellent vegetarian protein made from the soybean is tofu or soy cheese. Occasionally, the soy substitute meats are permissible.

With your protein dish, serve a small raw salad. Vary this from day to day. It is good to have a sulfur vegetable (cabbage or onion family) along with proteins to help drive the nerve fats to the brain. The two cooked vegetables can be of any of the non-starchy type. Remember the value of greens and eat plenty of them.

Your beverage may be a broth or soup; vary beverages with all the different herb teas, whey, raw milk or buttermilk.

It is permissible to have a health dessert at this protein meal, although the idea is not highly recommended. Fresh raw fruit is best.

You may exchange your noon meal for the evening meal, but follow the same regime. This is sometimes a good idea, especially if you have trouble getting to sleep. Starches predispose one to sleep more than proteins which are more stimulating.

No matter how wonderful the dinner, remember if you are emotionally upset, chilled, overheated, ill or lacking the keenest desire for plain food, miss the meal! That will do you more good.

When you plant good seed in well-mineralized soil, the result is healthy, hardy plants, free of disease and resistant to insects. In the same way, when you put a wholesome balance of foods into bodies with good digestion and assimilation, you get people free of disease and resistant to the various disturbances that come to the average person who lacks a balanced diet. Fresh juices are wonderful and essential foods that I consider necessary in any balanced food regimen.

Juices feed the tissues, energize the body, help prevent disease and add vitality and sparkle to wellness! Now that you know the "whys" and "wherefores," do yourself a favor and make juicing and juices a natural and regular part of your lifestyle! You'll be glad you did!

If You've Enjoyed Reading This Book . . .

Vibrant Health From Your Kitchen—One of Dr. Jensen's latest and greate books. In this book, he teaches the basics of health and nutrition. A food guide for family health and well-being. The reader learns how proper food can overcome certain mineral deficiencies, allergies and build immunity.

Food Healing for Man—Experiences are recounted in Dr. Jensen's work with both humans and animals. The book is a comprehensive layman's gui to the healing power of foods elaborating on nutritional deficiencies. Lists factors required for correcting body ailments. A study is made of why foo heal and the reason for supplements.

Nature Has A Remedy—Solutions applying nature's restorative powers are discussed. A nature encyclopedia covering hundreds of ailments. Teaches methods of taking care of various symptoms encountered with diet, water treatments, physical exercise, climate, environment and others.

Tissue Cleansing Through Bowel Management—Toxic-laden tissues can become a breeding ground for disease. Elimination organs, especially the bowel, must be properly taken care of. This book tells the reader how. Bowel management through a balanced nutritional program with adequate fiber in the diet and regular exercise can often do wonders. A special 7-da cleanse will bring back energy, regenerate tissues and allow good food to l nature do its healing work.

Unfoldment of the Great Within—This new book presents some of the teachings of Dr. V.G. Rocine, together with Dr. Jensen's thoughts and philosophy. In learning ease of mind, we begin to push disease out of our bodies. We should know how to start a new life and new day to become a wiser, healthier and better person.

Chlorella, Jewel of the Far East—Chlorella is a complete food. It is possibly the most thoroughly researched food of our time. One day man wi learn to live in harmony with nature. Then we will see a great restoring work being done on this planet, but until that day comes, chlorella is one o the most effective foods to protect us against the toxic effects of pollution.

Herbs: Wonder Healers—Herbalism is at least 5,000 years old, and the effects of many herbs have been carefully documented, especially in China Health is found in herbs more specifically than in all the other foods we usually purchase. More and more people are using herbs to help reverse an prevent ailments and diseases. Don't take anything for granted about herbs. Get your copy of this wonderful book; read it, and know your herbs.

Foods That Heal—In the first half of this book, Dr. Jensen focuses on the philosophy and ideas of Hippocrates, the brilliant work of Dr. V. G. Rocine, and concludes with a look at his own pioneering work in the field nutrition. The second half is a nutritional guide to fruits and vegetables.

Check at your local bookstore for information on Dr. Jensen's books and food products; if they cannot supply them, you may order directly from ou office. For a *free* catalog of all his books and supplies, you may write to:

Dr. Bernard Jensen
24360 Old Wagon Road
Escondido, CA 92027